IDENTITY THEFT

SOMEONE IS WATCHING YOU

AMERICA'S LATEST "RAGE"

momentum media
a division of VideoPlus, Inc.

VideoPlus

Published by Momentum Media, a division of VideoPlus, Inc.

To order additional copies of this book, please call 1.800.388.3884.

momentum media
a division of VideoPlus, Inc.

VideoPlus
200 Swisher Road
Lake Dallas, Texas 75065
U.S.A.
800.752.2030
Tel: 490.497.9700
www.videoplus.com

Printed in the United States of America.

Designed by Momentum Media, a division of VideoPlus, Inc.

ISBN 0-9672855-1-8

TABLE OF CONTENTS

INTRODUCTION

Identity Theft? "Nah, it could never happen to me," you may say to yourself. "I mean, what are the chances? I'm very careful with my personal information."

That's what every victim mentioned in this book once thought, if they thought about it at all. But it *did* happen to them and their lives were turned upside down, resulting in unforeseen expense, humiliation, and severe mental anguish. As they suffered with the realization they'd been personally violated, the last thing they wanted to face were the countless hours trying to straighten things out. But they had no choice if they were to recover even a shred of their dignity. Regardless what the numbers show, for the victims, the chances of identity theft turned out to be 100 percent.

You say you're careful? Well, let's see: How many times have you disposed of items containing personal information such as credit card statements, solicitations for credit, even utility bills, without destroying them first? Maybe you've used a personal computer at a trade show or library.

When dining out, and without giving it a second thought, have you handed over your credit card to a waiter you've never seen before and allowed him to slip away for a few minutes to "process it?" What do you really know about that person besides the "Todd" on his nametag? Do you know if he's in debt up to his ears? Are you sure the restaurant owner will even be able to find him the next day?

Are you sure *you* haven't already been victimized? Are you absolutely sure?

The truth is, while we go about our everyday business, identity theft is fast becoming one of the most insidious threats faced by our citizens and our economy. Just last year, more than 200 phony ID dealers in New York were arrested for operating six fake "identity mills" containing more than 2,000 forged documents. The fact that they got caught sounds like a victory for the "good guys," don't you think? Sure, but as those scam merchants were shut down, no doubt the vermin who avoided capture scattered and opened new ID mills or launched other insidious scams. Who knows? Your name might be on their list.

Criminals often have more on their minds than making a little quick cash. Identity theft has been implicated in crimes ranging from international drug trafficking to terrorism. In 2002, an FBI agent testified before a congressional subcommittee that Al Qaeda members in Spain used stolen credit and telephone cards and phony travel documents, including passports, to open bank accounts and to pay for travel and communications.

Each story described here is true. In many cases we only reveal partial names. After living their personal nightmare, some victims of this heinous crime are too embarrassed to be completely identified. For others, as they say, once bitten...

CHAPTER I

IDENTITY THEFT: STEALING OUR MOST PRIZED POSSESSION

When We Least Expect Trouble

Life was good for Mark, a top executive with a major securities firm. That is, until one fateful afternoon. Upon leaving work that day—a day he'll never forget—the police met him head-on, forced him face-down on the floor, slapped on handcuffs and searched his office and car for weapons, all in front of his shocked staff. What heinous crime had Mark committed? Nothing. Instead, Mark was a victim of identity theft—a crime that took root in the 1990s and has spiraled upward ever since. The sad fact is that Mark was arrested for crimes committed by someone who stole his name.

Fortunately, at the police station Mark was cleared after the police compared him to a photo and fingerprints of the true criminal. But that didn't mean Mark's nightmare was over. Since the felon exploiting Mark's identity skipped town—and the police did not have his real name—the authorities weren't in any hurry to correct the criminal records. Although Mark now has a certificate of clearance, arrest records (which are now transmitted nationwide) still show up with Mark's name and Social Security number. Sadly, this has proven to be a continuing disaster for Mark's career and personal life.

Identity theft is a multi-faceted crime packaged in countless shapes and forms. At its core, it occurs when someone uses information they acquire about an individual without permission—such as a Social Security number—to represent themselves as that person for fraudulent purposes.

For example, the criminal might obtain credit cards and loans in someone else's name with no intention of paying the bills. They might open utility accounts, rent an apartment, get a cell phone, even purchase a car or a home in their name. Identity thieves can even commit the unthinkable as in Mark's case: commit a crime in someone else's name, leaving the innocent, unsuspecting victim saddled with a criminal record.

A BIG Problem Growing Bigger

Identity theft is a rapidly growing problem. According to a survey released in September 2003 by the Federal Trade Commission (FTC), over the past five years, 27.3 million Americans had their identities stolen. Last year alone, nearly 10 million people were victims of identity theft. The FTC statistics mean nearly one in 10 Americans were victimized in the past five years. Surprisingly, nearly four out of 10 victims did not report the crime to any agency, the survey found. The FTC study was based on a random survey of approximately 4,000 adults.

"These numbers are the real thing," said Howard Beales, director of the FTC's Bureau of Consumer Protection, in a news release. "For several years we have been seeing anecdotal evidence that identity theft is a significant problem that is on the rise. Now we know. It is affecting millions of consumers and costing billions of dollars."

"This survey is proof positive that we must act quickly to stem the growing tide of identity theft by preventing identity thieves from getting hold of personal information—especially Social Security numbers—and enhancing penalties for those who misuse them," said Rep. E. Clay Shaw Jr. (R-Fla.), chairman of the House Ways and Means Subcommittee on Social Security.

The Gartner Group paints a similarly bleak picture, according to a study it recently conducted based on surveys completed by 2,445 U.S. households. They estimate seven million U.S. adults, or 3.4 percent of U.S. consumers, were victims of identity theft during the 12-month period under study—a 79 percent increase over the 1.9 percent rate they reported the previous year.

A recent survey by *Privacy & American Business,* a publication of the Center for Social & Legal Research, says the odds are even greater you'll be a potential identity theft victim. They estimate one in six adults have had their identities used by someone else since 1990. One in six! That could be someone on your street, in your apartment complex, in your Super Bowl pool, or sitting in the same row as you at a PTA meeting. Could it be you? Do you even know?

Hassles for the victim don't end when the problem is reported, the FTC survey found. Victims aren't responsible for paying the thief's expenses, but all identity theft victims pay $500 on average to clear their name. Victims of the most serious theft pay an average of $1,200, but costs decrease the sooner the theft is discovered.

Clearing a victim's name also takes time. Victims spend about 30 hours resolving the problem, with victims of the most serious crimes spending about 60 hours restoring their credit.

But even if you aren't a victim, you pay for it. While identity theft hits the victims the hardest, costing them $5 billion in out-of-pocket expenses, the FTC reports identity theft cost business and financial institutions nearly $48 billion. Do you think the companies are absorbing these costs, maybe writing them off? More than likely they're passing them on to their customers in jacked up prices or fees.

Could This Be *You*?

At least in the sad tale above, Mark avoided jail. **"At least,"** you say? The fact is that other victims of identity theft have fared far worse. Consider the case of Steven Benke of Portage, Indiana.

According to a news account in the *Gary Post-Tribune,* Mr. Benke had his identity stolen after misplacing his Indiana driver's license in May 2000. Somehow, Carter Metheny, of Michigan City, stumbled across it and used the name and address to obtain a new license containing his own picture and physical description. Metheny then passed bad checks he endorsed with Mr. Benke's name in Porter,

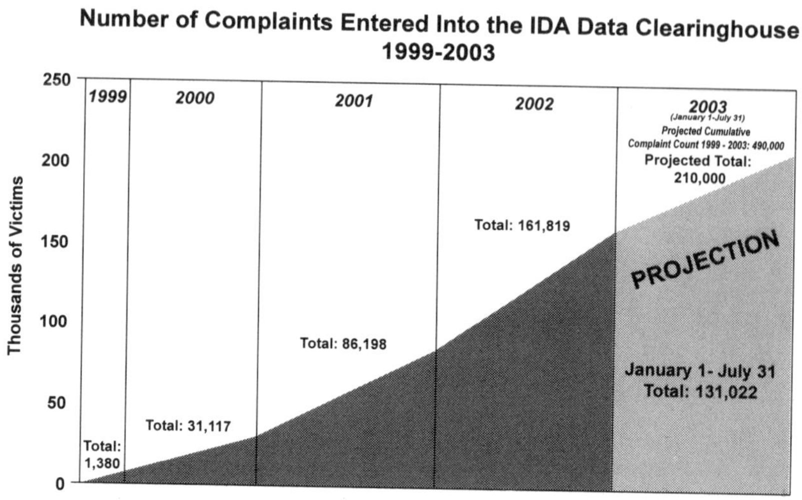

Source: Federal Trade Commission Report, September 2003

LaPorte and other counties in Indiana to obtain cash and merchandise by producing the driver's license with Steven Benke's name.

Eventually, the *real* Steven Benke landed in the Porter County Jail where he insisted he was innocent. On numerous occasions, he begged authorities to compare his signature to the handwriting on the forged checks, according to court documents. His claims, though, fell on deaf ears.

After nearly eight months, Mr. Benke was transferred to the LaPorte County Jail to face charges stemming from numerous other check forgeries. Several weeks later, he persuaded LaPorte County Deputy Prosecutor Thomas Alevizos to look into the matter.

"I called the Porter County prosecutor's office and they said he was telling them the same story," Alevizos told the Indiana newspaper. "Every place I turned it seemed like this guy was telling the truth."

Alevizos said he went to the Indiana Bureau of Motor Vehicles where he uncovered two driver's licenses that had been issued to Benke that same year. One license contained Mr. Benke's photo while the other displayed a picture of a man later identified as Carter Metheny.

Eventually, all of the charges against Benke were dismissed. "The guy spent nearly one year in jail falsely accused before they found out it was Metheny," said Alevizos.

"His voice wasn't heard because of other people who are guilty and say they are not," said David Sirugo, who was Mr. Benke's former public defender in LaPorte County. But his ordeal wasn't over. Later on, Mr. Benke had theft charges leveled against him in Porter County as a result of Metheny's criminal rampage. Metheny was arrested about a year later, charged with theft-related crimes. At the time, he was expected to receive a six-year prison sentence.

The Benke-Metheny case is not the only one of its kind. Recently, Derek Bond, a 72-year-old British man, was imprisoned for two weeks in South Africa after the FBI wrongly arrested him as a wanted fugitive. He was freed when the real fugitive was collared in Las Vegas. The U.S. Attorney's Office believes this crook had been using Bond's identity as far back as 1989.

In a similar situation, Malcolm Byrd was arrested several times, had his driver's license revoked twice, lost pay while sitting in jail, was eventually fired from his job and almost had his children taken away by child protective services—all because a criminal continued to use his identity.

Simple, Everyday Mistakes We All Make

Every day, without giving much thought, we perform our daily rituals. Maybe we write a check at the grocery store, charge tickets for a show or a ball game, rent a car, search and buy merchandise online, mail tax returns, call home on a cell phone, schedule a doctor's appointment, pay bills, order new checks, or apply for a loan or a new credit card. Most of us don't give these everyday transactions a second thought. But lurking in the shadows someone else may be after the information we so readily give out.

Let's face facts. Every day we share personal information about ourselves with others. It's so routine that we may not even realize we're doing it. Each contact and transaction requires us to share personal information: our bank and credit card account numbers, our income, our Social Security number, and our name, address and phone numbers. Once a resourceful identity thief gets hold of even one piece of your personal information, he or she can use it without our knowledge to commit fraud or theft.

The grim numbers tell the tale. Overall, the number of people who discovered misuse of their personal information has increased 41 percent, according to Betsy Broder, FTC assistant director of planning and information. Crimes involving opening new accounts and other frauds—which the FTC considers the most severe category of fraud—grew 17 percent.

It's all too easy for criminals to acquire the personal information they seek—particularly Social Security numbers. The FTC said thieves often get hold of personal information by stealing credit and bank cards, stealing or forwarding mail, rummaging through trash, using personal information shared on the Internet, fraudulently obtaining a credit report, or buying information from employees at businesses with financial or personal information.

One way of obtaining this information is by stealing a wallet or purse. The thief then either uses the information or provides the contents to a crime ring.

Once pilfered, Social Security numbers can be used to apply for credit and even give a criminal access to another person's credit report, credit card numbers, date of birth and driver's license numbers.

Careless handling of information by businesses we all deal with is one reason such information is easy to come by. Long after we leave their store or office park, our transaction records, applications and others documents are often thoughtlessly tossed in the trash without shredding them. Sometimes, dishonest employees pilfer computer files and personnel records.

TEST YOUR ID THEFT POTENTIAL

Take the following quiz about your personal habits. Do you:

1. store your personal information in a secure location in your home, especially if you have roommates, employ outside help or are having service work done in your home?
2. know the information security procedures in your workplace? Who has access to your personal information?
3. pay attention to your billing cycles and follow up with creditors if your bills don't arrive on time?
4. keep your purse or wallet in a safe place at work and know where they are at all times?
5. tear or shred your charge receipts, copies of credit applications, insurance forms, physician statements, checks and bank statements, expired charge cards that you're discarding, and credit offers you get in the mail?
6. carry your Social Security card in your wallet or purse?
7. give out personal information on the phone, through the mail or over the Internet when you haven't initiated the contact or aren't sure you know who you're dealing with (identity thieves may pose as representatives of banks, Internet service providers—also called ISPs—and even government agencies to get you to reveal your Social Security number, mother's maiden name, account numbers and other identifying information)?
8. use easily available information for your passwords such as your mother's maiden name, your birth date, the last four digits of your Social Security number or your phone number, or a series of consecutive numbers?
9. deposit outgoing mail in your own unsecured mailbox rather than a post office collection boxes or at your local post office?

If you answered "No" to questions 1 through 5, or "Yes" to questions 6 through 9, you are a prime candidate for identity theft!

Avivah Litan from the Gartner Group said many companies don't fully appreciate the seriousness or scope of the problem. "Many banks, credit card issuers, cell phone service providers and other enterprises that extend financial credit to consumers don't recognize most identity theft fraud for what it is," said Litan. "Instead they mistakenly write it off as credit losses, causing serious disconnects between the magnitude of identity theft that innocent consumers experience and the industry's proper recognition of the crime. This causes a disincentive to fix the problem with the urgency it requires."

Consider your own experiences. How many retailer clerks check your signature when you buy something? Few, if any, right? Either the companies don't instruct sales clerks to verify signatures on credit cards and credit card slips, or tell them not to for fear of "offending" good customers. And if it is company practice to have clerks ask for additional identification or to verify a signature, how many managers observe whether their clerks actually bother?

Think about it: Have you ever been asked for a second form of identification when a clerk wasn't sure about your identity when using a credit or debit card? Have you even had a clerk scrutinize your photo on your driver's license when paying by personal check?

If you order by mail or on the Internet, do you know if the company makes it a common practice to call the customer's registered home number, especially on phone orders? If someone tells them they have moved or the information doesn't match what's in the files, is it their procedure to contact you for verification?

Unfortunately, law enforcement doesn't investigate many of these type crimes. The sad fact is that there are just too many identity theft cases for them to handle and they just don't have the personnel or time to treat them as priorities. Frankly, law enforcement agencies are much more concerned and busy with other property and violent crimes such as breaking and entering, mugging, and robbery by gunpoint and bank thefts. Meanwhile, more and more criminals and organized crime rings are moving to identity theft.

INTERNET FRAUD STATISTICS

Total Loss Overall: $14,647,933
Average Loss: $468

2002 Top 10 Frauds

Online Auctions	90.0%
General Merchandise	5.0%
Nigerian Money Offers	4.0%
Computer Equip/Software	0.5%
Internet Access Services	0.4%
Work-at-Home Plans	<.1%
Information/Adult Services	<.1%
Travel/Vacations	<.1%
Advance Fee Loans	<.1%
Prizes/Sweepstakes	<.1%

Payment Methods Overall

Credit Card	34.0%
Money Order	30.0%
Check	14.0%
Debit Card	7.0%
Bank Debit	6.0%
Cashiers Check	3.0%
Cash	2.0%
Wire	1.0%
Other	3.0%

Initial Contact Overall

WWW	94.0%
Email	6.0%

Ages of Victims Overall

Under 20	3.0%
20-29	25.0%
30-39	28.0%
40-49	25.0%
50-59	14.0%
60-69	4.0%
70+	1.0%

Source: National Consumers League

CHAPTER II

WHO ARE THE VICTIMS?

Anyone can be a victim. Victims of identity theft come from all walks of life, occupations, income levels, and age, and they live in different size cities and towns in all 50 states. Sometimes simply having your name in a computer database can be enough. Consider these recent revelations:

- A computer breach allowed hackers to view eight million credit card numbers in the system of Omaha-based processing company Data Processors International. The card companies affected—Visa, MasterCard, and American Express—claimed no information was used fraudulently, yet Gartner Financial Services predicts at least 1 percent of those accounts—some 80,000 consumers—can expect to become targets of fraud as a result.
- More than 55,000 students, former students and employees of the University of Texas had their identities compromised when a hacker broke into the UT system and gained access to their names, Social Security numbers and e-mail addresses last February. "We flat out messed up on this one," said Dan Updegrove, vice president of UT's Information Technology.
- In 2002, online merchant Guess Jeans was caught with their proverbial "pants down" when a 19-year-old novice programmer, testing the site's security before buying a pair of jeans, broke in and retrieved 200,000 customer names and credit card numbers, despite the site's claim of being "secure." A Guess spokeswoman says they've zipped up their security since then.

Why Me?

The fact is, identity theft is an equal opportunity crime. Victims include teachers and principals, nurses and doctors, secretaries and CEOs, police officers, construction workers, retirees, students, and yes, even employees of district attorney's offices. Many celebrities have found out the hard way they are not immune.

In January 2003, a Sacramento, CA man was convicted of using Tiger Woods' identity to apply for credit cards and accrue about $17,000 in unpaid expenses. Prosecutors say Taylor used Woods' real name, Eldrick T. Woods, to apply for credit cards and purchase televisions, stereos, a used luxury car and services.

The "real" Mr. Woods testified that he never accrued expenses such as renting a rental truck in the Sacramento area or applying for a credit account at a local furniture store. Taylor's defense attorney, James Greiner, told the jury that it was ridiculous to think that anyone would believe his client was one of the world's most recognizable celebrities. Maybe…but someone did!

The following March, Abraham Abdallah was arrested by the New York Police Department and has been charged with attempted grand larceny in the first degree and possession of forged devices. Abdallah is accused of masterminding a scam to steal identities by using computers in a Brooklyn library to obtain credit records of chief executives and celebrities.

Authorities say Abdallah used the Web to steal money from the financial accounts of celebrities and business executives he may have found on the *Forbes* list of the "400 Richest People in America." Before he was caught, Abdallah stole money from Oprah Winfrey, Steven Spielberg, George Lucas, Martha Stewart, Ross Perot, Ted Turner, investors George Soros and Warren Buffett, and many other prominent executives.

According to a report in the *New York Post* and other New York newspapers, Abdallah, who worked as a busboy in a New York restaurant, allegedly duped credit companies into providing credit histories of the celebrities by sending them forged document requests on the stationery of leading investment banks, including Merrill Lynch and Goldman Sachs. He then apparently used the data to gain access to the celebrities' credit card numbers and brokerage accounts.

Using Web-based e-mail services available through computers in a branch of the local lending library, Abdallah allegedly made many requests to transfer funds from the existing accounts of the targeted people to phony accounts he had constructed. Abdallah may have successfully employed his ruse for as long as six months.

Abdallah also apparently used a Web-enabled cell phone and fax and virtual voice mail to make his requests seem more legitimate. He would create voice mail accounts in the area codes of his victims and then access them from New York. Callers, thinking they were leaving a message for Microsoft co-founder Paul Allen in Seattle, for example, would have heard a greeting (in Abdallah's voice), and Abdallah could have checked any messages left at that number.

Police detectives also claim Abdallah used a sophisticated set of mail drops to pick up his loot, sometimes using multiple couriers to take one package to its eventual destination, and monitoring the whereabouts of his packages sent to him via Federal Express and UPS.

According to the *Post*, the use of Web-based e-mail also led to Abdallah's downfall when he requested the transfer of more money than existed in the Merrill Lynch account of Thomas Siebel, founder of Siebel Systems, an e-commerce software provider.

The NYPD gradually unraveled the electronic trail left by Abdallah and nabbed him in dramatic circumstances after a sting operation, with the arresting officer diving through the sun roof of Abdallah's car to handcuff him. It was only after the arrest, law enforcement authorities say, that they discovered Abdallah's dog-eared and heavily annotated copy of *Forbes*, marked up with addresses, phone numbers, bank account numbers, Social Security numbers, and more information about the well-known people on the list.

We, The Victims

While each identity fraud case is unique, the victim's story is usually the same. Most receive little to no help from any of the authorities that issued the identifying information to them in the first place, including credit card companies, the Social Security Administration and the Department of Motor Vehicles. Many victims also say they don't receive much assistance from banks and credit card companies. They describe difficulty even reaching someone at the credit card companies, and tell how some creditors simply refuse to believe them—as if they're the criminals.

Across the nation, many police and sheriff's departments won't issue a police report to the victims—something victims need to prove their innocence to creditors. It's also typical for them to find flagging their credit report for fraud doesn't always stop the impostor from opening new credit accounts. Adding insult to injury, victims also have to put up with abusive collection agencies, which threaten them with repossessing their houses and cars.

Cleaning up the mess is a time-consuming task for the victims. Many end up taking days or weeks off work so they can make the necessary phone calls, write the letters and have affidavits notarized. According to a report from the California Public Interest Research Group (CalPIRG), the typical identity-theft victim spends 175 hours actively trying to resolve the problems caused by the theft. Problems include clearing up credit reports, filling out and submitting affidavits and dealing with lawyers.

If the victim is a member of your staff, you may lose hundreds of productive hours while your employee tries to straighten out their personal nightmare, and their problem, indirectly, becomes yours. The financial costs can be great as well, as victims must deal with a constant barrage of legal fees, phone calls, and miscellaneous expenses. Some victims end up saddled with the problems from identity theft for up to 10 years.

Privacy Violated, Independence Snuffed

There are also emotional tolls. Victims say they feel violated, vulnerable and very angry. Victims have used the word rape to describe how they feel.

"I felt totally helpless," Landon Browning, an engineer in San Francisco who fell victim to an identity thief last year told *ABC News* in a story on identity theft. "I never knew when something new might spring up. I was totally depressed about it."

"It was as horrible feeling," says Robert, a Web developer in Washington, D.C., who asked that his last name not be used. "You feel violated."

For some people, the experience can threaten more than just their bank account. "It almost tore apart my marriage," Robert Calip, a victim from Washington State told *CBS*. "Things were so bad that at one point my wife and I were on the verge of divorce. We were really at our wits' end."

Privacy Rights Clearinghouse, a non-profit consumer information and advocacy program based in San Diego, CA, reports it's not unusual to counsel—and console—victims who are weeping, or close to tears, because they can't stop what's happening to them. Then there are senior citizens who are frightened they will lose their life savings and their homes.

Is it any wonder why victims feel violated, helpless and angry? In the aftermath of their identity theft, they are often unable to rent an apartment, get a job, obtain a mortgage or buy a car, because someone else's bad credit history is hounding them. The entire burden of this crime is placed on the shoulders of the victims.

In one case Privacy Rights Clearinghouse knows about, a perpetrator was a major drug dealer who was using the identity of a high-tech company president. In the aftermath of "his" crime, the executive, who often travels out of the country, now has to carry a letter from law enforcement explaining he is not the drug dealer, since it had become routine for him to be pulled in for inspection every time he came back to the U.S. Recently, law enforcement agents from another state entered his bedroom in the early morning hours and tried to arrest him at gunpoint. He was able to eventually prove his innocence, but it took some doing.

Victims quickly learn they must be savvy and tough. To clear things up they must be assertive with the credit card and banking industries and officials. Unfortunately, many people find they are not equipped to deal with the problems this crime brings upon them: maybe English is not their first language, or they cannot communicate at the level of complexity that the problem requires. Others are semi-literate or illiterate and can't write the necessary letters. Unfortunately, there isn't enough consumer assistance for victims of identity theft.

CHAPTER III

BAND-AID REMEDIES?

To some degree, awareness of identity theft has increased over the past five years, primarily because of media coverage and alarms triggered by consumer advocates. As a result, some legislative and regulatory attention has been given the issue. There is a federal law on the books, the "Identity Theft and Assumption Deterrence Act." It makes identity theft a federal felony when someone knowingly uses the identification of another person with the intention to commit any unlawful activity under federal and state law.

Wisconsin Congressman Jerry Kleczka would like to take the law a step further and has introduced a bill (H.R. 1450) that, among other things, prohibits the commercial acquisition or distribution of Social Security numbers without the holders' consent and limits their use as personal identification numbers.

But while there is a heightened awareness among lawmakers that something must be done, so far, little of substance has been accomplished. In recent years, other identity-theft bills were introduced in the Senate but have either languished or been watered down. Political pressure from the credit industry makes it doubtful any bill restricting the sale of personal information will become law. According to the Privacy Rights Clearinghouse, identity thieves are rarely apprehended and sentenced. If they are, penalties are minimal and rarely include jail time. Community service and parole are common.

Compounding the problem, identity theft frequently crosses jurisdictional boundaries with the crimes often occurring outside the city or county in which the victim lives. Under those circumstances, where does the individual report the crime?

Making matters worse, many states do not have specific identity theft statutes. Even when such a statute exists, the definition of identity theft often varies from jurisdiction to jurisdiction and the format of crime reporting can easily cause cases to "fall through the cracks."

HAS THIS EVER HAPPENED TO YOU? YET?

You receive a phone call or letter stating you have been approved or denied credit for accounts you never requested.

You no longer receive your credit card statements, or you notice that some of your mail seems to be missing.

Your credit card statement includes charges for things you know you never bought.

A collection agency tells you they are collecting for an account you never opened.

CHAPTER IV

THE AGE OF MISUSED INFORMATION

Information about us is gathered and disseminated—both with and without our knowledge—from the time we're born until the day we pass away. Computers, networks and the Internet have increased the amount of personal information about us and reside in far-flung databases. Computers have made information gathering faster, and it's easier to disperse that information from one corner of the globe to the other. Very little regulation controls what happens to this personal information, and too often it is sold to anyone who has the means to purchase it to do with it whatever they want.

In the past, taking someone's identity or creating a new one meant using their passports or birth certificates and pretending to be this new person, according to Chris Cherrington, an analyst at research firm, Frost and Sullivan. "To steal someone's identity today no longer requires forged birth certificates or smudged photographs in driver's licenses but a smattering of technical knowledge," he said.

The major law enforcement agencies whose job it is to investigate identity theft crimes in the United States say the Internet has dramatically affected the way they do business. "[The Internet] has changed the entire landscape of law enforcement," says Bruce Townsend, special agent in charge of the Financial Crimes Division of the Secret Service. "It's been a major challenge for us to deal with the cyber age."

This challenge comes with significant costs: Not only must agencies like the Secret Service upgrade their systems to keep up with rapidly changing technologies; their staffs must also be well versed in the techniques and lingo of the cyber world. "Today," said Townsend, "all new recruits get a badge, a gun and a laptop."

According to the FTC, of the roughly 25,000 complaints received for 2000, 25 percent were related to online fraud and deception.

Dr. Neil Barrett, technical director at security consultancy IRM, explained that the crime is moving to the online world in two different ways: "You can either create an online personality by masquerading as someone else, or you can start to use someone else's existing details as your own." Experts agree the Internet is an ideal channel for those who wish to create multiple identities because users can interact without proof of real physical presence.

Adrian Wright, director of IT security at *Reuters U.K.*, said the lack of necessary physical presence could create a way in for the criminal regardless of where the victims live. "The amount of identity verification information needed in an online transaction is very little: birth dates, mothers' maiden names, addresses and a password, which can all be easily guessed," he said.

If It's Not Nailed Down

Law officials say the crime is remarkably easy to perpetrate. "It's incredibly easy," said security expert John Vranesevich. "Even the most novice user can get online and with a little bit of teaching could [commit identity theft] in an hour."

All that is required is snippets of information about its rightful owner, said Betsy Broder of the FTC. In many cases, this information can be readily found online via various data services like U.S. Search or Net Detective, or even offline with the phone book.

Armed with such information, an identity thief can open a bank account, take out a loan or order credit cards—all of which can now be done from the anonymity of a personal computer.

Compounding the ease of the theft is growing demand for the stolen data: There is a vast virtual black market on the Web, using tools like Internet Relay Chat (IRC) and Instant Messenger (IM), where individuals buy and sell stolen credit card and Social

Security numbers with the same ease with which they might buy or sell merchandise on eBay.

Since the Internet is a global phenomenon, the traffic in stolen identity flows effortlessly across borders. “Today, a hacker in Moscow can break into a system in Singapore, steal credit card numbers and transfer them via the Internet to a co-conspirator in Buenos Aires, where merchandise will be purchased that is transshipped and sold on the streets of Miami,” said Townsend.

Townsend said the current identity theft hot spots are Eastern Europe and Southeast Asia, where the level of education and technical sophistication is high, and where tracking down and prosecuting criminals can be very problematic.

“Card details are easily obtainable from hard copy printouts or by telephone or directly from a user’s PC,” explained Winn Schwartau, a security expert and author.

A former hacker, named “Jericho,” told the Web site *Silicon.com* that current personal information protection methods used by banks simply act as an invitation to criminals: “Most credit cards are protected by four digit PINs which are very easy to guess with the help of a basic PC. You can even find software programs designed to do this.”

CHAPTER V

SEVENTEEN WAYS TO STEAL YOUR IDENTITY

The Categories

Identity theft can be divided into three broad categories:

1. "True name" fraud occurs when someone uses your personal information to open a new account.
2. In an "account takeover," the person gains access to an existing, legitimate account: *yours.*
3. Someone uses your personal information to avoid prosecution commits "criminal" identity theft.

Often these schemes overlap and have common elements. The end result is the same. An innocent person is ripped off.

The List

Here's a list of the most frequent ways identity theft happens. There are many more schemes than these, and new ones are concocted every day. Unfortunately, many victims haven't a clue as to how their identifying information was obtained by the impostor.

1. Mail Theft
2. Dumpster Diving: One Man's Trash…
3. Counterfeit Credit and Debit Cards
4. Employee Theft: Access to Company Data
5. Stolen or Lost Wallets and Purses
6. Account Takeover

7. Shoulder Surfing
8. Friends and Relatives
9. Revenge
10. Burglary
11. Pretext: Phone Scams
12. Skimming
13. Phony Bankruptcy
14. Scanning the Newspaper
15. Social Security Number Theft and Misuse
16. Raiding Old Computers
17. Computer Fraud

1. Mail Theft

> *"In November 2000, I found out that someone used my information to obtain a cell phone. Since then, I've been living a nightmare. My credit report is a mess. It's a full-time job to investigate and correct the information."*
>
> From a consumer complaint to the FTC

Mail theft, a principal way of obtaining identifying information, is accomplished when people leave their paid bills in an unlocked mailbox for the carrier to pick up rather than dropping them off at the Post Office. Maybe you're the type of efficient person who puts his or her mail out and raises the red flag in the evening before going to bed. If enough people on your street do this, your neighborhood becomes a virtual midnight shopping mall for identity thieves.

Identity thieves particularly seek out new credit cards sent through the mail. How often are we aware we're due for a new card from our friendly credit card company (who sends it via regular mail, without a return receipt requested)? Even if we're waiting for a new one, it only takes a day or more for a criminal to run up thousands of dollars worth of charges on our cards before we realize it's been pilfered.

In the change-of-address routine, a thief fills out a change-of-address card so the victim's mail is diverted to the thief's drop box. Then the thief obtains bank statements and credit card bills or pre-approved offers of credit containing enough information to impersonate the victim. The Postal Service recently began verifying change of addresses in order to make this more difficult, but too often, crooks are one step ahead of any remedy.

2. Dumpster Diving: One Man's Trash...

Jane and her husband, both professionals living in Michigan, were about to buy their first home when the loan officer informed them that their credit was overextended. Someone in Texas had used Jane's name and Social Security number to obtain numerous credit cards, a BMW, health care and a mortgage. It took two years to clean up the mess and purchase a new home. The nightmare has finally ended, but the fear of future problems is ever present.

Sometimes, credit card slips and loan or credit applications are fished from the trash. By filling out a credit application, an impostor can change the victim's name and identifying information and have it sent to another address. The major credit card issuers say they are now more wary of changes of address, but their efforts are not foolproof.

Unfortunately many businesses, banks, mortgage companies and restaurants do not shred documents pertaining to us. Credit card slips, photocopies of checks, private phone numbers, prescription forms, duplicate receipts and even employees' personal records and histories are being carelessly tossed out, there for the thief's taking.

It's an all-too-common practice for identity theft criminals to dig into trash cans behind retailers, doctors' offices, video rental stores, retailers and large department stores and mortgage brokers' offices, bringing up handful after handful of sensitive information. It's all there for the taking; all the information an impostor needs to assume an identity and steal thousands of dollars in merchandise, cash and services.

But it's not always some two-bit criminal. Organized crime rings are also involved, using the information themselves or selling it on the black market.

Poor document handling often results from lack of awareness: the company does not establish secure methods of information disposal, and employees don't realize the serious implications of identity theft.

But we're also to blame. How often do we toss unwanted credit card solicitations right into the trash without even opening them? What about those blank checks our credit companies send to us in bunches to get us to draw down our unused credit limits? What do you do with those? Many of us just flip them into the trash without tearing them up first.

Again, if you're the efficient type, you might put your trash out the night before it's due to be collected. When you see your cans overturned in the morning and scattered around the yard, do you assume a cat or other animal did it? You might be right about the "other animal." But what you might not suspect is that it was due to a two-legged breed rummaging for information goodies and not for food.

3. Counterfeit Credit and Debit Cards

In February 2003, seven Floridians were indicted for using online Federal Court records to steal identities of prisoners and defrauding banks of more than $1.7 million. The defendants used the U.S. District Court's Internet-based PACER system and other means to acquire biographical and credit information for prisoners. "PACER" (Public Access to Court Electronic Records) is a computer program used by the administrative office of the U.S. courts.

The technology to make a counterfeit card is as close as your nearest electronics store and has evolved into Internet sites offering "free" cards. A counterfeit card is created when someone possesses your card number, and then uses the coding of your magnetic strip to create their own card with their own name printed on the front.

When you receive your monthly statement, to your dismay, you notice thousands of dollars of charges that you did not make. That is, if you're savvy enough to check your statement at all.

4. Employee Theft: Access to Company Data

John worked as a part-time bookkeeper for Dr. Stone, an ophthalmologist. John's job entailed accepting cash and checks from patients. He began to divert tens of thousands of dollars into a checking account in a neighboring town using Dr. Stone's name. He began to impersonate Dr. Stone and ordered eyeglasses and equipment for a new eye clinic using Dr. Stone's credit profile, license, etc. He hired staff and even continued to work as a part-time bookkeeper while diverting the funds he needed. Dr. Stone only learned of the business identity theft when John's business began to fail and creditors started to harass the doctor. Dr. Stone's reputation was destroyed and his quest to regain his credibility and sanity is ongoing.

Linda Goldman-Foley, director of VOICES (Victims of Identity Crimes Extended Services), a non-profit organization that publicizes identity theft awareness, points out many companies don't limit or control the number of people who have access to sensitive information and few have established data security procedures for each type of identifying documentation their employees handle.

Making matters worse, many companies don't have a process to screen employees who have access to personal information, especially part-timers. This includes out sourced employees who may be in the office unsupervised, including cleaning crews. When a company uses Social Security numbers for employee and customer identification and that information is not stored in a totally secure location, it could be a disaster waiting to happen.

Ms. Goldman-Foley knows this is true from personal experience. She became an identity theft victim when her employer used her personal data to apply for several credit cards and a cell phone.

Today's modern office technology—e-mail, voice mail, personal computers, cellular telephones, answering machines and other services—are neither private nor secure. Despite what many think, these are not reliable ways to transmit sensitive messages. In addition, many are lulled into a false sense of security thinking that "deleting" messages actually remove information from a hard drive. Messages people thought were deleted have been retrieved and used as evidence in lawsuits.

5. Stolen or Lost Wallets and Purses

Mary's purse was stolen while on vacation. When she got home she found several new credit cards in the mail, ones she never applied for. The bills followed several days later. The impostor had found her Social Security number on her health insurance card and used it to secure "instant" credit at various stores. He maxed out the accounts the day they were opened, leaving Mary to deal with the collection agencies.

Even if your wallet or purse is returned intact, there's no way to know whether someone copied your personal information.

6. Account Takeover

"My wallet was stolen in December 1998. There's been no end to the problems I've faced since then. The thieves used my identity to write checks, use a debit card, open a bank account with a line of credit, open credit accounts with several stores, obtain cell phones and run up huge bills, print fraudulent checks on a personal computer bearing my name, and more. I've spent the last two years trying to repair my credit report (a very frustrating process) and have suffered the ill effects of having a marred credit history. I've recently been denied a student loan because of inaccurate information on my credit report."

From a consumer complaint to the FTC

Account takeover is one of the most common forms of identity theft. It doesn't require the technology of a counterfeit card or the waiting time of a fraudulent application.

Account takeover occurs when someone acquires your personal information. Often they do not need your actual card number. Once the perpetrator has your information, he or she will contact your credit card company and change the address on your account.

Next, they call and report your card lost or stolen and request a new card replacement. The new card is then sent to the new billing address on the account. Voila! The criminal has successfully taken over your account.

Playing right along without their knowledge, companies often link PINs and other information to the new card automatically. The criminal can access cash, and sometimes even have access to the checking account information that you provided to your credit card institution. Despite all the new security measures that many card companies now have, account takeover incidents are on the rise.

7. Shoulder Surfing

"I applied for a loan in November 2000 and was told I had bad credit. I requested a credit report in November 2000 and found all sorts of crazy information on it. I'm single but was listed as married. When I renewed my driver's license by mail, I was surprised to find someone else's face on my license. This is a nightmare and requires a large amount of my time."

From a consumer complaint to the FTC

Without you realizing it, your phone conversations could be overheard while you're conducting personal business. Also, while you're focused on an ATM transaction someone could be zeroing in as you enter your PIN and you might not even know it. If you didn't notice that, is it likely you would notice if the same person followed you home to find out your address, adding to his other file of personal information about you?

8. Friends and Relatives

Charlie had his identity stolen when a friend of a landlord copied some information from an apartment rental form sitting on a desk. The impostor used that information, which included Charlie's Social Security and driver's license numbers, to get a duplicate driver's license and accumulate more than $50,000 in credit card bills. Then he used the victim's name when arrested by the police for drug smuggling. Charlie was forgiven all the debts but his name still is on a national crime register. He is forced to carry a letter of clearance with him wherever he goes to prove he is not the felon who used his identity.

Relatives or friends, roommates, acquaintances, acquaintances of acquaintances, household workers such as health care givers or spouses going through a bitter divorce can easily obtain a victim's Social Security number, driver's license number and credit card numbers. This is much more common than most people would believe.

"More than half of all identity theft—where the method of theft is documented—is committed by criminals [who] have established relationships with their victims, such as family members, roommates, neighbors, or co-workers," said Avivah Litan, vice president and research director for the Gartner Group.

9. Revenge

One of the ways for someone to get even after a falling out with a family member or well-known acquaintance is to steal their identity and damage their financial standing and reputation.

Take the case of Dana and David. They were married for 25 years, and both were physicians and business partners. Learning that David was having an affair with their receptionist, Dana asked for a divorce. David vowed that she would never get anything from the business.

Her husband had a great reputation and political influence and he began to use it to destroy Dana's life. While the divorce battle raged, Dana began receiving collection calls, money was stolen from her accounts, and she was billed for things she didn't order. Her phone was disconnected "by mistake" and her mail was stolen. One day, the FBI arrived at Dana's medical office and arrested her for writing painkiller prescriptions she had never authorized.

Dana went to trial with an attorney who didn't allow her to testify and didn't make a case that she had been framed (she later found out the lawyer was a friend of her ex- husband). She was convicted on a drug charge and is trying with a new attorney to get a new trial.

10. Burglary

A Texas man somehow obtained a woman's stolen driver's license and combined it with his state identity card, his name and picture, and her address and identifying information. Car thieves had stolen the woman's purse from her home. Someone used a credit card stolen during the break-in to run up $4,000 in purchases. Her husband had already cancelled the cards but he's worried someone might have collected other personal information in the theft. He hadn't known what had happened to his wife's license until a reporter told him that police found the missing license on a convicted thief, at 3 a.m. while investigating a suspicious car.

For those unfortunate enough to have their home burglarized, the reaction is usually the same: they check to see if cash, jewelry and other valuables have been stolen. What they don't typically check, though, is whether old checks, unused and activated credit cards, and those blank checks our credit card companies love to send us have been pilfered. Other things also forgotten—but not by crooks—are passports, Social Security cards, birth certificates and other forms of identification.

11. Pretext: Phone Scams

Pretexting is the practice of getting your personal information under false pretenses. Pretexters sell your information to people who may use it to get credit in your name, steal your assets, or to investigate or sue you. Pretexting is against the law.

Pretexters use a variety of tactics to get your personal information. For example, a pretexter may call, claim he's from a survey firm, and ask you a few questions. When the pretexter has the information he wants, he uses it to call your financial institution. He pretends to be you or someone with authorized access to your account. He might claim that he's forgotten his checkbook and needs information about his account. In this way, the pretexter may be able to obtain personal information about you such as your Social Security number, bank and credit card account numbers, information in your credit report, and the existence and size of your savings and investment portfolios.

There is a law against this practice. The Gramm-Leach-Bliley Act ("GLB") prohibits individuals from obtaining a customer's information from a financial institution or directly from the customer using false representations, fictitious documents or forgery.

Section 521 of GLB specifically prohibits the following practices when used to obtain customer information from a financial institution:

- Making or attempting to make a false representation or statement to an officer or employee of a financial institution;
- Making or attempting to make a false representation or statement to a customer of a financial institution; and
- Providing, or attempting to provide, a forged or fictitious document to an officer or employee of a financial institution.

For example, it is a violation of GLB to pose as a customer of a financial institution to obtain personal financial information, to deceive the customer into providing personal financial information to you or to provide a financial institution with a document known to be fictitious for the purpose of obtaining customer financial information. More on these scams later.

Keep in mind that some information about you may be a matter of public record, such as whether you own a home, pay your real estate taxes, or have ever filed for bankruptcy. It is not pretexting for another person to collect this kind of information.

12. Skimming

Kathryn Mangold, a manager at a hospital in London unknowingly became a victim if identity theft in April 2003, when a week after shopping in central London in the U.K., she received a letter from Barclaycard, Britain's biggest credit card company, which had issued her a Visa card. Although Ms. Mangold says she is careful with her cards, she was shocked to read that there had been abnormal activity on her account.

After speaking directly to the bank she found out that someone had gone on a shopping spree the weekend after her shopping trip and, using her card details, had spent the equivalent of more than $800 in a computer superstore and a toy store chain. Lucky for her, the bank acted quickly and canceled her account number.

Ms. Mangold was a victim of skimming or cloning: an escalating and highly effective form of credit card fraud. Her tale of woe was part of a story on skimming that recently appeared on *ABC News.*

Experts say skimming is one of the most difficult types of credit card fraud to prevent because the criminals work so fast that they leave almost no trace.

Skimming is costing credit card users around the world millions of dollars in phony charges, as stolen clones are sold and used in the U.S. and elsewhere. The practice took off in the United States several years ago and is beginning to approach the scale of fraud that plagued credit cards in the early 1990s before new precautions were taken, according to Gregg James, a special agent with the Secret Service's Financial Crimes Division in Washington.

As many as 10 to 15 restaurants a week across the United States are cited by industry sources as harboring skimmers, James told *ABC News.* "Any place you use your card, you could be a victim."

Here's how the scam works. Criminal gangs recruit gofers, who then find temporary work within restaurants, hotels and retail outlets. The recruits are given small, illicit, electronic devices known as skimmers that capture all of the credit or debit card's details in the few seconds that it takes to swipe the card through the machine.

When unsuspecting customers go to pay their bill, their card is first swiped through the legitimate credit card machine, but then, secretly, it is also swiped through the smaller skimmer machine.

The gofers then pass the gadgets on to counterfeiters, who pay them the equivalent of around $150 for their part in the crime. Once the details have been given to counterfeiters, they download the information on to a computer and make up a fake card. The "cloned" card is embossed with the details of the victim's credit card and passed on to gang members who, police say, may sell it for between $400 and $700, depending on the perceived credit limit.

Gold or platinum cards are normally targeted because of their higher credit limit, meaning the bank takes longer to realize there is a problem. And criminals spend, on average, about $2,800 per card, with large and frequent transactions typically over a two-day period before discarding the card, according to one expert.

While the whole process of getting a cloned card on to the streets can take less than a day, the customer is none the wiser, since his own his credit card is in his wallet. In fact, victims may not realize they've been taken until they check their statements at the end of the month. By that time the criminal has moved on and the electronic and paper trails are cold.

London police recently cracked a massive credit card fraud ring and earlier this year, two Russian nationals were sentenced to four years each and also served with a deportation order for their parts in the crime.

One of them, Vladimir Stronguine, distributed skimming devices and controlled a network of waiters working throughout London's restaurants. The second, Alexander Tanov, was the "card maker" who had turned his bedroom into a virtual credit card factory.

Tanov's equipment was capable of producing near perfect replicas of American Express, Visa and MasterCard credit cards. When confiscated, police found 500 credit card details on his computer—only one in five had been taken from cards issued by British banks; the rest had been lifted from cards issued across the United States and Europe.

At the time of the arrests, police found evidence of fraud totaling $300,000. Had the Russians been left to continue, authorities believe the operation would have resulted in losses of $7 million.

But while card details are often stolen in Britain, experts say the cloned cards are used all over, especially in the United States. New York is also considered a "hotbed" of skimming among U.S. cities.

"The rapid growth in counterfeit fraud is not a U.K.-based problem; it is a global problem," says Brian Moore of Europay, the European arm of MasterCard International. "Coupled with the fact that fraud is no longer an opportunist crime but an organized crime, people need to be very aware of where their card is at all times."

13. Phony Bankruptcy

This scam targets people whose home mortgages are in trouble. The scammers—running ads saying something like "Be debt-free in 12 months"—promise to take care of problems with mortgage lenders or to obtain refinancing for the victim. Sometimes they ask the victims to make mortgage payments directly to them. They may even ask victims to hand over property deeds. The scammers pocket all the money the victim has paid and file for bankruptcy in the victim's name, usually without the victim's knowledge. Victims lose their money and their homes and are left with a bankruptcy listed on their credit records.

14. Scanning the Newspaper

If you're looking for a loan, that official-looking newspaper advertisement you answer would not only avoid providing the money you seek but also drain your bank account. Recently, the Federal Deposit Insurance Corporation (FDIC) released a warning to consumers about bogus ads placed in small or community newspapers. "On face value, you would not know there was anything out of the ordinary," said FDIC Spokesperson David Barr.

The bogus ads offer mortgage, small business, debt or consolidation loans. The ads look real because they use the logos of real banks—but with different contact information. The contact numbers in the ads have been traced to prepaid cell phones.

Potential victims who apply for these bogus loans are asked to provide their Social Security numbers and are then told their loans have been granted. The scammers fax the victim a loan application, requesting bank account information and sometimes a copy of the applicant's driver's license and Social Security card. The scammer then asks for an advance payment through a Western Union wire transfer. Only when the fake loan never appears does the victim realize what has happened: that he's wired cash to a thief and his identity has been stolen.

"Most victims lost $500 to $800 dollars each," said Barr. But, another danger is the possibility for identity theft, which could lead to a much greater loss, he said.

The FDIC warns that you should be suspicious of any bank that requests you to wire money outside of the banking system or to what the scammers are calling a "third-party consultant."

"Banks tend to offer consumer loans directly," said Barr. "If you are asked to wire money outside of the bank or outside of the country that should raise some red flags."

Consumers should also be suspicious if the phone numbers in the ads are answered on a cell phone. According to the FDIC, the scammers are communicating with the newspapers through prepaid cell phones purchased in Canada. This scam is similar to an "advance loan" scam also being run out of Canada.

15. Social Security Number Theft and Misuse

"Tomorrow is Sunday so we won't get any notices, but I'm not looking forward to Monday's mail."
From a consumer complaint to the FTC

Social Security number theft can be accomplished by insiders, employees or temporary workers who have access to a computer terminal connected to one of the credit reporting bureaus. Going hand-in-hand with this type of access is the negligence of the company permitting unmonitored access. Insiders have also used access to personnel records to obtain Social Security numbers of identity theft victims.

The Privacy Rights Clearinghouse reports of a case where a member of a foreign-organized crime ring was employed temporarily at a very large corporation. He downloaded the employee list containing Social Security numbers. One by one the employees' identities were used for fraudulent purchases. The employees didn't know about it until they started sharing stories and learned that many of them had been victimized.

According to Edward Wabe, a Las Vegas-based security expert, "The Social Security number was never meant to be a universal identifier. In fact, it is really poorly suited to the task."

16. Raiding Old Computers

Two MIT graduate students, Simson Garfinkel and Abhi Shelat, recently bought 158 used hard drives from computer stores, small businesses and eBay, the online auction site. Many of the hard drives were physically damaged and/or had unreadable sections. Nevertheless, the pair managed to retrieve a lot of information from directories and files that had been deleted. Forty-two of the drives had what appeared to be credit card numbers. Garfinkel says they don't know for sure if they're working credit card numbers because that would have required trying to make a transaction.

One drive appeared to have been used in an Illinois ATM. Garfinkel says it had nearly 3,000 numbers that he suspects were ATM card numbers. It also contained account numbers and balances. He says no effort had been made to remove the drive's financial information. Another drive had credit card number and expiration information that Garfinkel says he believes was used for Internet purchases. "People are not generally aware that even after the computer says the information has been deleted, it can be recovered," says Garfinkel.

DO THEY REALLY NEED YOUR SOCIAL SECURITY NUMBER?

A number of federal laws and regulations require federal programs and federally funded activities to use Social Security numbers to enforce compliance with laws and determine eligibility for benefits. The Internal Revenue Service (IRS) uses Social Security numbers as taxpayer identification numbers. Employers and others making payments to individuals must include Social Security numbers in reporting payments to the IRS. Reportable payments include interest payments, employee wages, investor dividends, retirement benefits, cash deposits or purchases of more than $10,000 and annual mortgage interest payments of more than $600.

Taxpayers must include their Social Security numbers on income tax forms as well as the Social Security numbers of their dependents and ex-spouses who receive alimony. However, federal law neither requires nor prohibits many other uses of Social Security numbers by the public and private sector. Some businesses may ask you for your Social Security number to do a credit check, like when you apply for a loan, rent an apartment, or sign up for utilities. Sometimes they simply want your Social Security number for general record keeping. These auxiliary uses put consumers at risk of identity theft.

Banks often use the last four digits of Social Security numbers as the default personal identification number for ATM cards and telephone banking access. Many insurance companies use Social Security numbers as account numbers and print them on membership cards that must be carried by the health plan member. Most colleges and universities use Social Security numbers as student IDs, and grades often are posted using Social Security numbers. In some states, Social Security numbers are used as driver's license numbers.

If your financial institution, insurance company, motor vehicles department or school uses your Social Security number to identify you, you can ask to have it replaced with another account number, personal identification number or secret code. You don't have to give a business your Social Security number just because they ask for it.

To really get rid of something on your hard drive you have to go way beyond pressing the delete key. Joan Feldman, president of Seattle-based Computer Forensics, Inc., explains that when you delete a file, the computer's operating system marks the file with a symbol and, essentially, removes it from view. If you did a search for the file, it wouldn't show up, but it's still on the hard drive until it's been written over—several times—by other files.

"When the hard drive is completely filled and you can't save any more files, the operating system looks for a place where it can save a new file and goes to the location of that deleted file. It releases that space back to you," says Feldman. "But it's like a pencil mark on a wall that you cover with a coat of paint. You can still see the mark, so you cover it with another layer of paint and it's obscured some more. That process is called wiping, shredding or file wiping. In fact, it's adding layers of data on top of other data."

However, if you don't use a lot of graphics, video or music files, you may not run out of space, so your system may never need to write over data you deleted.

Computers retain about three times more information than the average user would suspect," said Feldman. "It's like a piece of black velvet in a lint factory. When you're on the Internet, stuff is being dumped to your hard drive like you wouldn't believe. When you use Word or Excel, they very often create multiple copies of the files you're working on. The end result is that little thing that's smaller than a paperback can contain much of your personal history for as long as you've owned that computer."

17. Computer Fraud

"I'm tired of the hours I've spent on the phone and all the faxing I've had to do. When will it be over?"
From a consumer complaint to the FTC

It's easy to become somebody else and have the IDs to prove it—especially if you're wired. That's the finding of a Senate subcommittee, whose members recently told senators how easy it is to get a fake driver's license, Social Security card or birth certificate on the Internet. Subcommittee members displayed some fake IDs obtained through Web sites—including some showing Sen. Susan Collins, R-Maine, the head of the subcommittee, as a reporter, a U.S. Army reservist and a student at Boston University. The fake credentials claimed she lived in Florida, Wyoming, Connecticut and Michigan.

Officials told the senators that nearly 30 percent of all fake identification documents currently come from the Internet, up from less than 5 percent just two years ago. During a five-month investigation, Collins's subcommittee turned up at least 60 sites selling fake identification or show people how to create it themselves. Where were they located? It's nearly impossible to tell since they don't give out locations. They could be anywhere.

Some of the counterfeit documents are of "shockingly high quality," with official-looking bar codes and holograms, said K. Lee Blalack, chief counsel and staff director for Collins' Permanent Subcommittee on Investigations.

"It will be no easy task to maintain the integrity of the identification documents on which both the government and private sector rely because of the new technology," Blalack said.

David Myers, fraud coordinator for the state of Florida, added, "Now that we're finding some that have a counterfeit magnetic stripe, it makes it very, very difficult for law enforcement to determine the counterfeit from the original."

Collins' staff subpoenaed documents and interviewed more than 40 witnesses in the investigation and worked undercover to buy high-quality false IDs that could be used to fabricate credentials for employment.

And they found the fake ID business could be profitable. Investigators found a 21-year-old student at Loyola University in Baltimore who generated more than $8,000 from 621 orders for fake IDs in two months, according to Blalack.

Thomas Seitz, a 23-year-old convicted felon awaiting sentencing for making fake IDs, said he used fraudulent documents to get $60,000 in car loans.

Seitz also described how easy it was to obtain personal information for the IDs online, which he started doing via a computer at a public library in Old Bridge, New Jersey. "I obtained, via the Internet, names, Social Security numbers and addresses of people by accessing files maintained as public record on the Securities and Exchange Commission Web site," Seitz said.

Data transferred across the Internet can be potentially intercepted during its journey because of the open nature of the Internet. Users must feel confident when revealing sensitive information, like credit card details, that this information will be kept safe and secure. Encryption technology, which renders data secure by turning it into an unreadable cipher, is fundamental to the development of e-commerce. However, Internet security is as much about policy as technology.

Hacking is broadly defined as the unauthorized use of computer and network resources. The term 'hacker' originally derives from the actions of often-gifted individual programmers, testing their skills and "hacking" into private and public database systems and computer sites. The "thrill" is to beat the security systems in place. Too often, though, the "payoff" is stealing your identity.

WHAT'S YOUR PASSWORD?

Most people choose bad passwords that are easily guessed. Ten of the most common passwords are: God, love, lust, money, private, QWERTY, secret, sex, snoopy, and, believe it or not, password.

How about at work? How secure is the information residing on your computer network? Consider these facts from recent news reports:

- According to the *Search Security Newsletter*, 60 percent of all corporate data assets reside unprotected on PCs.
- The *2002 Computer Security Institute/FBI Computer Crime & Security Survey* reports 90 percent of corporations and government agencies detected computer security breaches within the previous 12 months; 80 percent acknowledged financial losses due to these breaches.
- The same study shows the average financial loss from computer security breaches was over $2 million per company. The most serious financial losses occurred through theft of proprietary information.
- Also from the study, only 34 percent of organizations that have a security breach report the intrusions to law enforcement.
- In a recent survey by *Information Week* magazine, 4,500 security professionals revealed "enhancing network security" was identified as the top strategic security priority for companies, and was noted by respondents as increasing in importance.
- Sixty to 70 percent of attack vulnerability occur in the "people area"—customers and employees, for example—according to a study by *eWeek*.
- In another recent study, he OMNI Consulting Group reported network security breaches put 5.57 percent of a business's annual gross revenue at risk.

CHAPTER VI

SCAMS, SCAMS AND MORE SCAMS

"Phish" Stories

According to Internet Fraud Watch, one of the latest scams on the Internet are authentic-appearing e-mails requesting verification of financial information. Ironically, many such bogus e-mails prey upon consumers' fears of being exposed to fraud. They ask for updated credit card account information or other pieces of personal financial information and state that the consumer's account will be terminated in the near future if the information requested is not provided.

One recent fake appeared to originate from Citibank. The scam technique, nicknamed "phishing"—an obvious play on the word "fishing"—"spoofing, "brand spoofing," or "carding," this scam is causing so many problems that the FTC, the Federal Bureau of Investigation, the National Consumers League and Earthlink held a press conference recently in Washington, D.C., about the problem. "Bogus e-mails that try to trick customers into giving out personal information are the hottest, and most troubling, new scam on the Internet," said Jana Monroe, Assistant Director of the FBI's Cyber Division.

In this scam, the phisher sends out a legitimate-looking e-mail that claims to be from a company the reader—or phish—does business with and tells the reader that there is an account error, possible fraud or other problem with the account. The reader is asked to click on a link in the e-mail and enter account information on the linked Web site. The link takes the reader to a phony Web site that gathers the information and uses the information to drain the reader's bank account, charge up their credit card and possibly steal their identity.

Spammers mask their identities by using a wide array of computer servers, opening and closing their operations quickly and working outside the United States. All of this makes it more difficult for U.S. law enforcement to catch up with them.

Recently, Citibank reported that this scam was attempting to dupe their customers. "Citibank urges recipients of this e-mail to delete it immediately," says the Citibank Web site. "Citibank does not ask customers to provide sensitive information in this way. Don't reply to any e-mail that requests your personal information."

In the past, similar e-mails attempted to defraud users of eBay, PayPal, America Online, BestBuy.com, Discover Card, Earthlink and SonyStyle.com. Even people who do not have accounts with these companies may receive the e-mail because it is sent as spam to as many e-mail accounts as possible. All of these companies state they would never ask their customers for personal information in an e-mail.

In one variation, one gaining in popularity, scammers claim to be from the victim's credit card company, eBay or PayPal. In this identity rip-off the con artist sends a message that states that the company—a name you recognize—needs to verify the victim's account information to make sure it's protected. The scammers then use the information to make fraudulent charges to your account.

eBay posts on their site that they would never e-mail or call you to ask for account information; if you are registered, they already have it. However, eBay may send you an e-mail requesting that you change your password if they suspect fraud.

In July 2003, the FTC filed their first action against a suspected phisher, a 17-year-old California boy who allegedly used a page made to look like America Online to scam people out of their credit card numbers. If approved by the court, the teen will be banned for life from sending spam and will have to pay a $3,500 fine, the FTC said. Because of his age, his name was not released and officials said it is unlikely he will face criminal charges.

"This is the FTC's first law enforcement action targeting phishing. It won't be the last," said FTC Chairman Timothy Muris.

Internet Scams

Here's just a sample of scams that run rampant on the Internet.

FRAUDULENT E-MAIL TO CITIBANK CUSTOMERS

Claim: Citibank is sending out checking account suspension notices and asking customers to verify their acceptance of new terms and conditions.
Status: False.
Example: [Collected on the Internet, 2003, www.snopes.com]

> Your Checking Account at Citibank
>
> We are letting you know, that you, as a Citibank checking account holder, must become acquainted with our new Terms & Conditions and agree to it.
>
> Please, carefully read all the parts of our new Terms & Conditions and post your consent. Otherwise, we will have to suspend your Citibank checking account.
>
> This measure is to prevent misunderstanding between us and our valued customers.
>
> We are sorry for any inconvinience it may cause.
>
> Click here to access our Terms & Conditions page and not allow your Citibank checking account suspension.

Fraudulent requests for account number to PayPal customers

Claim: As part of regular security maintenance, Paypal needs you to resubmit your credit card and bank account information.
Status: False.
Example: [Collected on the Internet, 2003, www.snopes.com]

PayPal®

Dear PayPal Customer

PayPal is currently performing regular maintenance of our security measures. Your account has been randomly selected for this maintenance, and placed on Limited Access status. Protecting the security of your PayPal account is our primary concern, and we apologize for any inconvenience this may cause.

To restore your account to its regular status, you must confirm your email address by logging in to your PayPal account using the form below:

Email Address: __________

Password: __________

Bank Account

Enter Bank Account #: __________

Credit Card

Enter Credit Card #: __________

Exp. date 03 / 03

[Log In]

This notification expires March 31, 2003

Thanks for using PayPal!

This PayPal notification was sent to your mailbox. Your PayPal account is set up to receive the PayPal Periodical newsletter and product updates when you create your account. To modify your notification preferences and unsubscribe, go to https://www.paypal.com/PREFS-NOTI and log in to your account. Changes to your preferences may take several days to be reflected in our mailings. Replies to this email will not be processed.

If you previously asked to be excluded from Providian product offerings and solicitations, they apologize for this e-mail. Every effort was made to ensure that you were excluded from this e-mail. If you do not wish to receive promotional e-mail from Providian, go to http://removeme.providian.com/.

Copyright© 2002 PayPal Inc. All rights reserved. Designated trademarks and brands are the property of their respective owners.

FRAUDULENT SECURITY UPDATE TO EBAY CUSTOMERS

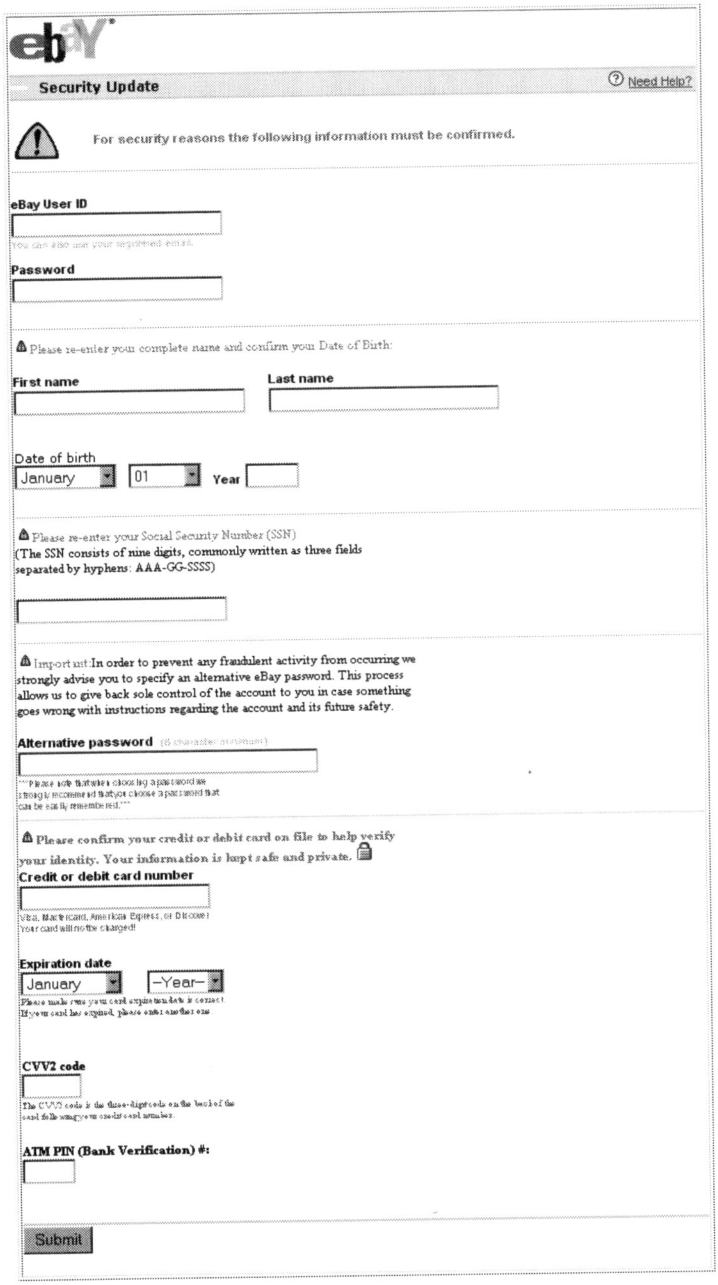
Security Update

Need Help?

For security reasons the following information must be confirmed.

eBay User ID

You can also use your registered email.

Password

Please re-enter your complete name and confirm your Date of Birth:

First name **Last name**

Date of birth January 01 **Year**

Please re-enter your Social Security Number (SSN)
(The SSN consists of nine digits, commonly written as three fields separated by hyphens: AAA-GG-SSSS)

Important: In order to prevent any fraudulent activity from occurring we strongly advise you to specify an alternative eBay password. This process allows us to give back sole control of the account to you in case something goes wrong with instructions regarding the account and its future safety.

Alternative password

Please confirm your credit or debit card on file to help verify your identity. Your information is kept safe and private.

Credit or debit card number

Visa, Mastercard, American Express, or Discover
Your card will not be charged!

Expiration date

January –Year–

Please make sure your card expiration date is correct.
If your card has expired, please enter another one.

CVV2 code

The CVV2 code is the three-digit code on the back of the card following your credit card number.

ATM PIN (Bank Verification) #:

Submit

Source: www.snopes.com

FRAUDULENT SCAM ALERT TO VISA CUSTOMERS

Claim: Phony e-mails purportedly from VISA's "Department of International Investigations" are luring gullible victims into divulging their credit card information to scammers.
Status: Undetermined.
Example: [Collected on the Internet, 2002, www.snopes.com]

Subject: VISA SCAM ALERT

SCAM ALERT: Visa USA Fraud Control has learned of a scam designed to obtain cardholders personal data and account information. Visa reports this activity in Canada, but suspects it may spread to the United States. A member/cardholder may receive the following letter:

VISA Department of International Investigations.

Dear ....,

We regret to inform you that your credit card is cancelled until further notice and this in accordance with article 205 of chapter 210 of the international fraud department. We suspect that your card has been involved in criminal activity. In the next two days one of our investigators will contact you on the phone and proceed to verify your customer information. The violation of this law is a serious criminal act and could bring you before the courts. Your bank will not be able to assist you until our investigation is over. We are advising you that our offices are open 24 hrs a day. For further information on the matter you may visit our web site at HTTP://WWW.VISAFRAUD.COM

Yours truly,
XXXXX....
Director, Visa Corporation

Visa reports it is not sending this letter. Do not respond to this letter or any subsequent telephone calls. Also report to Visa USA Fraud Control, if you receive this or a similar letter. Contact SCAM Alert at 1-800-637-2676, email us at scamalert@cunamutual.com, or fax the information to 608-231-8987.

NIGERIAN SCAM

Claim: A wealthy foreigner needs your help moving millions of dollars from his homeland to yours and will reward you with a hefty percentage of this fortune if you agree to assist him.
Status: False.
Example: [Collected on the Internet, 2000, www.snopes.com]

REQUEST FOR URGENT BUSINESS RELATIONSHIP

FIRST, I MUST SOLICIT YOUR STRICTEST CONFIDENCE IN THIS TRANSACTION. THIS IS BY VIRTUE OF ITS NATURE AS BEING UTTERLY CONFIDENTIAL AND 'TOP SECRET'. I AM SURE AND HAVE CONFIDENCE OF YOUR ABILITY AND RELIABILITY TO PROSECUTE A TRANSACTION OF THIS GREAT MAGNITUDE INVOLVING A PENDING TRANSACTION REQUIRING MAXIIMUM CONFIDENCE.

WE ARE TOP OFFICIAL OF THE FEDERAL GOVERNMENT CONTRACT REVIEW PANEL WHO ARE INTERESTED IN IMPORATION OF GOODS INTO OUR COUNTRY WITH FUNDS WHICH ARE PRESENTLY TRAPPED IN NIGERIA. IN ORDER TO COMMENCE THIS BUSINESS WE SOLICIT YOUR ASSISTANCE TO ENABLE US TRANSFER INTO YOUR ACCOUNT THE SAID TRAPPED FUNDS.

THE SOURCE OF THIS FUND IS AS FOLLOWS; DURING THE LAST MILITARY REGIME HERE IN NIGERIA, THE GOVERNMENT OFFICIALS SET UP COMPANIES AND AWARDED THEMSELVES CONTRACTS WHICH WERE GROSSLY OVER-INVOICED IN VARIOUS MINISTRIES. THE PRESENT CIVILIAN GOVERNMENT SET UP A CONTRACT REVIEW PANEL AND WE HAVE IDENTIFIED A LOT OF INFLATED CONTRACT FUNDS WHICH ARE PRESENTLY FLOATING IN THE CENTRAL BANK OF NIGERIA READY FOR PAYMENT.

HOWEVER, BY VIRTUE OF OUR POSITION AS CIVIL SERVANTS AND MEMBERS OF THIS PANEL, WE CANNOT ACQUIRE THIS MONEY IN OUR NAMES. I HAVE THEREFORE, BEEN DELEGATED AS A MATTER OF TRUST BY MY COLLEAGUES OF THE PANEL TO LOOK FOR AN OVERSEAS PARTNER INTO WHOSE ACCOUNT WE WOULD TRANSFER THE SUM OF US$21,320,000.00 (TWENTY ONE MILLION, THREE HUNDRED AND TWENTY THOUSAND U.S DOLLARS). HENCE WE ARE WRITING YOU THIS LETTER. WE HAVE AGREED TO SHARE THE MONEY THUS; 1. 20% FOR THE ACCOUNT OWNER 2. 70% FOR US (THE OFFICIALS) 3. 10% TO BE USED IN SETTLING TAXATION AND ALL LOCAL AND FOREIGN EXPENSES. IT IS FROM THE 70% THAT WE WISH TO COMMENCE THE IMPORTATION BUSINESS.

PLEASE,NOTE THAT THIS TRANSACTION IS 100% SAFE AND WE HOPE TO COMMENCE THE TRANSFER LATEST SEVEN (7) BANKING DAYS FROM THE DATE OF THE RECEIPT OF THE FOLLOWING INFORMATIOM BY TEL/FAX; 234-1-7740449, YOUR COMPANY'S SIGNED, AND STAMPED LETTERHEAD PAPER THE ABOVE INFORMATION WILL ENABLE US WRITE LETTERS OF CLAIM AND JOB DESCRIPTION RESPECTIVELY. THIS WAY WE WILL USE YOUR COMPANY'S NAME TO APPLY FOR PAYMENT AND RE-AWARD THE CONTRACT IN YOUR COMPANY'S NAME.

WE ARE LOOKING FORWARD TO DOING THIS BUSINESS WITH YOU AND SOLICIT YOUR CONFIDENTIALITY IN THIS TRANSATION. PLEASE ACKNOWLEDGE THE RECEIPT OF THIS LETTER USING THE ABOVE TEL/FAX NUMBERS. I WILL SEND YOU DETAILED INFORMATION OF THIS PENDING PROJECT WHEN I HAVE HEARD FROM YOU.

YOURS FAITHFULLY,

DR CLEMENT OKON

NOTE; PLEASE QUOTE THIS REFERENCE NUMBER (VE/S/09/99) IN ALL YOUR RESPONSES.

Tax Rebate Scam

Since many parents looked forward to receiving their Advance Child Tax Credit, con artists having been calling American homes, promising to speed up the rebate process for a fee of $39.99, to be placed on a credit card. While the tax credit of as much of $400 per child issued by the government is real, the promise of the cons is not.

Voice Mail Scam

If you have a four-digit password on your voice mail, you may be vulnerable to hackers who could rack up long-distance charges on your bill. According to a warning issued by AT&T, these hackers dial until a voice mail message picks up, then dial away until they figure out the code. When they do, they change the outgoing message to say the phone accepts third-party calls. Then they charge long-distance calls to your telephone account. You won't know anything has happened until you listen to your outgoing message or get your bill. To protect yourself, AT&T recommends changing your voice mail code to a six-digit number or using an answering machine.

Online Auction Scams

There are many, many scams at online auctions. First is the escrow scam: the seller requests that you use a certain escrow company to pay for your item. But the escrow service is a fake in cahoots with the seller—and you quickly discover you're out all your money.

Second is the phantom seller with the great (fake) bid history. When you try to check up on this seller's history you will see nothing but praise—too bad all the praise has been posted by the seller and his friends. Again, you're out all your money.

This next one is for sellers: the fake cashier's check. This scam bears a strong resemblance to the infamous Nigerian letter scam so many of us have received. Here's how it works: You get an order from someone who wants to pay by cashier's check, usually outside of the United States. You deposit the check. The bank tells you the check has cleared and you send the items. Several days later, you'll find out the check really didn't clear and the bank holds you responsible for the balance.

In another twist, you'll get a cashier's check for more than the amount you requested. The buyer will ask you to refund the difference. You do—then the cashier's check bounces and the bank holds you responsible for the balance.

Fake Job Boards

The last thing someone looking for a job in a depressed market needs is to have his dwindling bank account dwindle even more with the unwanted help of others. Recently, the job search Web site Monster.com found it necessary to send out a warning to its users: don't give out personal information after it discovered identity thieves were placing fraudulent job postings to trick job seekers into giving out personal information. The cons contact the job seeker and ask for personal information such as Social Security number and bank account information, supposedly for the human resources department. The moral of the story: *never give out personal information online.*

If The Price Is Too Good To Be True...

One flourishing identity theft scam can be found on Web sites selling high-demand items at a much lower price than offered by legitimate companies. The victim is told to pay nothing until the item is received. The scammer then uses the victim's name, along with an unlawfully obtained credit card number belonging to another person to buy the item at a legitimate Web site. Once that Web site ships the item to the victim, the victim, believing that the transaction is legitimate, then authorizes his credit card to be billed to the scammer or sends payment directly to the scammer.

Phony Sweepstakes And Prizes

In this scam, the perpetrators tell victims they have won a prize or sweepstakes. Victims are then told they need to send the company taxes on the winnings or purchase a product to receive the prize. It's illegal for a company to require purchasing a product or paying a fee to win or claim a prize. And taxes are never sent to the awarding company—only to the IRS.

Some scammers will instruct the victim to share bank account, Social Security or credit card numbers. No legitimate sweepstakes company will ask for this information. These scammers steal the victim's identity and empty their bank accounts, make charges on the victim's credit card or open accounts in the their name.

Some con artists use company names that are identical or very similar to well-known, legitimate sweepstakes operators. Internet Fraud Watch says doubting consumers should contact the real company to verify the call, e-mail or letter.

Another sweepstakes scam reported by the Better Business Bureau involves an advance. These scammers give advances on the promised winnings to build trust. They send a check as an advance on the winnings, instructing victims to cash it and then wire payment to them for taxes, bonding or some other phony purpose. After victims wire the money, the deposited check finally bounces because it turned out to be an elaborate fake. Now the scammers have the payment, and the victim owes the bank the amount withdrawn.

OCC ALERT 2002-3: FICTITIOUS IRS FORMS & BANK LETTERS

ALERT 2002-3
OCC ALERT

Comptroller of the Currency
Administrator of National Banks

Subject: Identity Theft Description: Fictitious IRS Forms and Bank Letters

TO: *Chief Executive Officers of All National Banks; All State Banking Authorities; Chairman, Board of Governors of the Federal Reserve System; Chairman, Federal Deposit Insurance Corporation; Conference of State Bank Supervisors; Deputy Comptrollers (districts); Assistant Deputy Comptrollers; District Counsel and Examining Personnel*

RE: WARNING--Circulation of Fictitious IRS Forms and Bank Letters

Attached are samples of a fictitious document that is not a genuine IRS Form and a fraudulent letter addressed to a bank customer purporting to be from the customer's bank.

Some of your customers may be the unwitting subjects of a new fraud scheme that uses fictitious IRS Forms and fraudulent bank correspondence. These incidents are not limited to the customers of small community banks. Documents like those attached are being circulated nationwide in an attempt to **steal your customer's identity and money** by having your customer disclose personal and banking information. Accordingly, when the perpetrator of the fraud contacts your bank in person, telephonically or through electronic means, they have all the necessary customer information to appear credible.

You should advise any of your customers that have filled in and returned the fictitious form via the fax number, mail service, or any other means to promptly notify all financial institutions with whom they do business. We also suggest that you advise your customers to immediately do the following:

1. Contact the fraud department of each of the three major credit bureaus and report that his/her identity has been stolen. Also, consider placing a "fraud alert" on your file and request that no new credit be granted without prior approval.

	Equifax	**Experian**	**Trans Union**
Address	P.O. Box 740241 Atlanta, GA 30374-0241	P.O. Box 2104 Allen, TX 75013	760 Sproul Road P.O. Box 390 Springfield, PA 19064-0390
Order Credit Report	1-800-685-1111	1-888-EXPERIAN (397-3742)	1-800-916-8800
Report Fraud	1-800-525-6285	1-888-EXPERIAN (397-3742)	1-800-680-7289

2. For any accounts that have been fraudulently accessed or opened, contact the security department of each affected creditor or financial institution. Consider closing these accounts. Also, on any new accounts you open, consider using a password, but do ***not*** use your mother's maiden name.

3. File a report with your local police department or the police where the identity theft took place. Retain a copy of the police report in case your bank, credit card company, or others need proof of the crime at a later date.

4. Contact the Internal Revenue Service to report the incident using the following toll-free hotline number: 1-800-829-0433.

If a customer has received this fictitious form but did not complete and return it, any information which they have concerning this matter should be brought to the attention of the Internal Revenue Service at the same toll-free number listed above.

Additional sources of information for your customers on what to do if they are a victim of identity theft, and the precautions to take to prevent becoming a victim, can be found at the Federal Trade Commission's Web site:

http://www.consumer.gov/idtheft/victim.htm

and the OCC's Web site:

http://www.occ.treas.gov/idtheft.pdf

If you have additional questions, please contact the supervisory office responsible for your bank or:

Mail:	Office of the Comptroller of the Currency Enforcement & Compliance Division 250 E Street, SW, Washington, DC 20219
Fax:	(202) 874-5301
Internet:	http://www.occ.treas.gov
E-mail:	occalertresponses@occ.treas.gov

Brian C. McCormally
Director
Enforcement & Compliance Division

Attachments: Customer Letter
Application Form

Source: Comptroller of the Currency Administrator of National Banks
(www.occ.treas.gov/altlist02.htm)

OCC Alert 2002-4: Organized Gang and Teller Collusion Schemes

ALERT 2002-4

OCC ALERT

Comptroller of the Currency
Administrator of National Banks

Subject: Identity Theft Description: Organized Gang and Teller Collusion Schemes

TO: Chief Executive Officers of All National Banks; All State Banking Authorities; Chairman, Board of Governors of the Federal Reserve System; Chairman, Federal Deposit Insurance Corporation; Conference of State Bank Supervisors; Deputy Comptrollers (districts); Assistant Deputy Comptrollers; District Counsel and Examining Personnel

RE: Identity Theft and Embezzlement in connection with Outside Parties

The Office of the Comptroller of the Currency (OCC) has been advised of fraud schemes involving organized gangs and newly hired bank tellers. Organized gangs are aggressively recruiting bank tellers to cash forged savings account withdrawals from customer accounts, and to cash stolen United States Treasury checks. Tellers are reportedly being paid several hundred dollars per transaction to assist in this fraud scheme.

Federal law enforcement officials have learned that organized gangs are using coercion and threats of bodily harm to persuade individuals to assist them in the fraud scheme. In some cases, tellers already employed by financial institutions are being recruited. More commonly, individuals are being encouraged by gang members to apply for teller positions at financial institutions for the sole purpose of providing access to the institution's operating systems and customer access information. Typically, the gang member provides stolen information to the teller who keys the information into the bank's automated systems so it will appear as if customer visited the teller window. The perpetrators are careful to keep amounts under supervisory approval limits. As a result, detection is delayed until the victimized customer reports the fraud.

Organized gang activity has become more sophisticated and the sphere of influence of some gangs has expanded geographically. National banks should exercise care and due diligence in their hiring practices, and periodically evaluate internal controls over the teller area. National banks should also file a "Suspicious Activity Report" (SAR), if the situation warrants.

Any information that you have concerning this matter, or any questions about OCC's SAR requirements, should be brought to the attention of :

Mail: Office of the Comptroller of the Currency
Enforcement & Compliance Division, MS 8-10
250 E Street, SW, Washington, DC 20219
Fax: (202) 874-5301
Internet: http://www.occ.treas.gov
E-mail: occalertresponses@occ.treas.gov

Brian C. McCormally
Director,
Enforcement & Compliance Division

Source: Comptroller of the Currency Administrator of National Banks (www.occ.treas.gov/altlist02.htm)

OCC Alert 2002-6: Fictitious Bank Correspondence and Fraud Reporting Forms

Bankof YOUR BANK NAME

Credit Card
Consumer Fraud Control

Phoenix,

Fax

April 18, 2002

CUSTOMER
12345 Street

HOMESTEAD, FL

Re: Product credit card XXXX-XXXX-XXXX

Dear CUSTOMER:

Thank you for notifying us about the suspected fraudulent account that was opened in your name. To help prevent additional charges from occurring, we have closed this account.

To begin our investigation, we have enclosed a fraud questionnaire form. Please return the completed form in the self-addressed, postage paid envelope within ten days of receipt of this letter.

Thank you for your patience and cooperation in resolving this situation. If you have any questions please contact us at 1-800-

Sincerely,

Fraud Applications
Phone: (800)
Fax:

USA ← Unauthorized USE of trade Marks →

FROM ________________

NO POSTAGE NECESSARY IF MAILED IN THE UNITED STATES

BUSINESS REPLY MAIL

FIRST-CLASS MAIL PERMIT NO SAN FRANCISCO, CA

POSTAGE WILL BE PAID BY ADDRESSEE

BANKCARD SERVICES

FRAUD CONTROL

PO BOX

Bank Fraud Questionnaire

Account Number: X________________

Name on Account: ________________

Address on Account: ________________

Your Full Name: ________________

Current Address: ________________

City, State, and Zip: ________________

Length of Time at current Residence: ________

Home Phone: ( )________ Work Phone: ( )________

Social Security Number: ____-____-____

Previous Address: ________________ From: Month/Year ________

________________ To: Month/Year ________

Please list the name(s) and relationships of any person(s) residing with you at any of the above address(es):

Name ________________ Relationship ________________

Name ________________ Relationship ________________

Who do you suspect completed the application for credit in you name? ________________

Explain why you suspect them: ________________

Do you have any information that could assist us in contacting the suspect? (i.e. address, social security number, phone number, drivers license number-state issued, employer, etc.)

____

Have you spoken to the suspect regarding this matter? Yes ________ No ________

Can we contact them? Yes ________ No ________

Has a police report been filed? Yes ________ No ________

If yes, report number: ________ Police Department: ________

Telephone Number: ________ Detective or Officer Name: ________

Signature: ________________ Date: ________

*Signature: ________________ Date: ________

* Please be sure to include a copy of your drivers license and social security card when you return this form.

Source: Comptroller of the Currency Administrator of National Banks (www.occ.treas.gov/altlist02.htm)

CHAPTER VII

WHILE YOU WERE SLEEPING: THE IDENTITY MILL NIGHTMARE

The reach and diversity of the Internet has accelerated fake ID problems. Many criminals—and potential criminals—use the Web to talk about how to make a fake ID, and numerous sites "sell" fake identification cards.

Not so long ago, an Internet business that bragged about the "high quality" of the templates it sold to help produce false identity documents was ordered to halt the sales by a U. S. District Court at the request of the FTC. "There is no legitimate use for defendant's templates and programs," the FTC complaint filed in U.S. District Court stated.

The FTC complaint stated Jeremy Martinez of Tarzana, California, doing business as Info World, maintained Web sites, including one located at a site called "newid" that sold 45 days of access to fake ID templates for $29.99. The site contained "high quality" templates for the creation of fake California, Georgia, Florida, Maine, Nevada, New Hampshire, New Jersey, Utah, Wisconsin and New York driver's licenses. It also contained a birth certificate template, programs to generate bar codes—required in some states to authenticate driver's licenses—and a program to falsify Social Security numbers.

The FTC said Martinez was deliberately marketing his site to consumers who were surfing the net to find fake ID documents. A recent Congressional investigation brought attention to this problem and some Web sites have disappeared as a result. But others still remain. In addition, some of the Web sites warn that, ironically, some of their competitors may take a customer's money but not deliver the fake ID. Recently, the FTC took action against six people who were allegedly selling fake international driver's licenses through the Web.

Illegal immigration also is an area where fake identification cards are an underground business. Law enforcement officials, for instance, have seen an increase in the sale of fake IDs at flea markets.

Not surprisingly, colleges and universities still are a hotbed of fake identification cards. Police have taken action at Iowa State University, Purdue University and the University of California San Diego, to name a few, to break up fake ID card "mills." Often these mills can sell hundreds of cards, often at the beginning of a semester.

CHAPTER VIII

SPECIAL VICTIMS OF IDENTITY THEFT

Preying On The Elderly

According to the most recent FTC data, incidents of identity theft of those over the age of 60 increased by 218 percent. Older people make appealing financial targets because they typically have higher credit lines, greater home equity and more financial resources than younger populations. However, almost 66 percent of those 65 and older did not report the crime (younger victims did better, with only 17 percent of those 18 to 24 years old not reporting the crime).

If more people had reported the crime, retired Army Lt. Colonel John Stevens might have been forewarned. At a Senate Special Committee on Aging, he told U.S. ranking member Senator Larry Craig how an identity thief bought four cars and other items worth over $113,000 using his name. "After a lifetime of integrity, all of a sudden I was essentiality being accused of embezzlement and treated like a deadbeat," Stevens said. He said he has spent over $6,000 in legal fees trying to repair his credit and the people he believes stole his identity more than five years ago have not yet been prosecuted. Speaking on behalf of both himself and his wife, Stevens said, "Our feelings can be simply expressed by quoting a line from the movie *Network:* 'We're mad as hell and we're not going to take it anymore!'"

Compounding their problems, many elderly victims don't even have a touch-tone phone to alert the credit bureaus to fraud alert. Once the credit reports are received the information is often confusing. Many letters and affidavits must be sent to creditors, and without a computer, this is a huge task. Furthermore, many companies take advantage of the elderly thinking they don't really know what's going on. On many occasions bank have refused to reinstate accounts that were fraudulently tampered with, telling the elderly victim nothing could be done.

Some of the elderly are special targets. For example, hoax letters were mailed to elderly African-American people across the South, telling them they may be eligible for $5,000 in slave reparations or Social Security reimbursements. According to Arkansas Attorney General Mark Pryor, the letters, which include requests for Social Security numbers, were apparently part of a scam aimed at stealing people's identities and running up credit bills under their names. "What they are really trying to get is personal information from seniors," he said.

The slave reparations letter, in all capital letters on plain white paper, is targeted at those born "prior to the year of 1928 and of the black ethnic race." It suggests that the federal government is seeking individuals entitled to payments under a supposed "Slave Reparation Act."

The other letter is targeted at people born between 1917 and 1926. It says these "notch babies" are due $5,000 each because of a glitch in Social Security collections. "People born between those years may indeed be getting less Social Security money because of the way the retirement program was set up, but Congress has not been able to fix the error," Pryor said.

The letter plays on those congressional attempts, saying, "There is a measure attempting to be passed, but you must be registered in order to receive it."

Both letters, which were also circulated in African-American churches and senior centers, instruct people to submit their name, address, telephone number and Social Security number to the National Victims Registrar in Washington, D.C. The payments would be added to future government benefits checks or issued in a lump sum, the letters promise.

Preying On The Young

Although it's rare, child identity theft is a particularly insidious form of a proliferating crime. While adults are far more likely to be identity theft victims—only 2 percent are children—experts worry that as the crime continues to grow and perpetrators get wilier, kids will become more vulnerable. Congress, considering changes to the nation's credit system, is mulling new protections from identity theft for children.

Some experts fear child identity theft is under-reported because victimized youngsters often do not discover the crime for years—until they are young adults applying for a driver's license, a college loan or a first credit card.

"We can have a ton of kids who've been victims of identify theft and don't even know it," said Linda Foley, co-executive director of the Identity Theft Resource Center in San Diego. And when the perpetrator is a family member, children and young adults may hesitate to report the crime, not wanting to get a family member into trouble.

Take the case of Michelle Thibodeau and her 16-year-old son when she took the youngster to get his learner's permit in Worcester, Massachusetts. To their shock, they learned he already had a driver's license. "I looked at them like they were nuts," Ms. Thibodeau told *ABC News*. "We went and talked to a manager, who pulled up [my son's] driver's license file on the computer," Thibodeau said. "The photo on the screen was of his father."

Ms. Thibodeau says her ex-husband, James Johnson, who is currently in a state prison in Massachusetts on unrelated charges, stole their son's identity years earlier to get a license. Soon after, the teen received a notice from the state Department of Revenue alerting him that he was delinquent in his child support payments—money his father apparently owed for other children, Thibodeau said. Thibodeau informed the department of her son's situation.

Still, when the boy got a job as a grocery store bagger, the Department of Revenue seized part of his paycheck. Thibodeau called the agency again, but part of her son's tax return was taken as well.

Ms. Thibodeau tried her best to clear her son's name. She contacted the Social Security office, the IRS tax fraud hotline, the FTC, local police and the district attorney's office. But bureaucratic roadblocks slowed her down. And Johnson, incarcerated for seven years, had outrun Massachusetts' six-year statute of limitations on identity theft and couldn't be charged, prosecutors told her.

Unlike adults, children don't leave trails of personal information that can be lifted by hackers from databases or thieves rooting through garbage cans. Instead, adults usually victimize children with access to their fledgling identities: their Social Security numbers and/or birth certificates. Perpetrators might be strangers who work at a health clinic, insurance company or school, or any other place that requires access to a child's personal information. Illegal aliens may purchase a child's information from traffickers who target youngsters particularly because it will take years before the crime is noticed.

Sadly, though, children are often victimized by people they know well, such as family and close friends with bad credit or suspended licenses who may see a new beginning for themselves in the juvenile's pristine record.

"It's often a family member or someone who knows the child," said Jim Vaules, fraud consultant for LexisNexis Risk Management and a former FBI special agent. "Most newborns are getting Social Security numbers. The person will assume the identity of the youngster for purposes of getting a clean record."

Young adults are particularly at risk, experts say, because more people have access to their information. Amy Gergely, now a spokeswoman for Intersections, Inc., a Virginia-based company that provides credit counseling, was herself a victim, just before her 18th birthday.

"It was after I applied for my first credit card to take to college. As far as I can tell, it was a former work colleague from my summer job who stole my employment information and got credit in my name," Gergely said.

"Minors nearing college age and beginning to establish a credit record are at far more risk of identity theft, in our opinion, than 3-year-olds, due to their new, sparkling clean credit records and lack of credit education," she said.

Credit education can also help consumers protect themselves, and their children, from identity theft, experts say.

Surveys show that young adults, at least, have little understanding of the credit process. More than 60 percent of young adults, ages 18 to 24, say their knowledge of credit reports are fair or poor, according to a report by the Consumer Federation of America.

In the most extreme cases of abuse, children end up having to change their Social Security numbers. But experts say that should be avoided if possible. It's like entering the government's witness protection program—any record of one's former identity is erased. And, teens with a brand-new Social Security number may run into problems when it comes to getting college loans, for example. That's what Michelle Thibodeau's son ended up facing.

About a year into his fiasco, the office of Thibodeau's congressman, Rep. James McGovern, D-Mass., helped her apply for a new Social Security number for her son. The application review would take weeks, and the number might not ever get changed, Thibodeau was told. But when a local newspaper columnist featured Thibodeau's case in a story last June, mother and son started seeing results.

"The article put a fire under people's butts," Thibodeau said. "The tax money that was intercepted was returned, and his Social Security number was changed a week after the article ran."

CONCLUSION

So Much Needs To Be Done

While the Identity Theft and Assumption Deterrence Act offers some help much more needs to be done before the average, law-abiding citizen can feel secure. While the law is an improvement, in order to make a dent in identity theft, the practices of the credit industry must change dramatically.

Don't hold your breath.

Identity theft is at near epidemic proportions primarily because of the careless practices of the credit granting industry. Until laws create incentives for how they conduct business, the crime of identity theft will continue to climb.

Again, don't hold your breath.

Without external pressure from legislators and industry associations, financial service providers (FSPs) may not have the sufficient incentive to stem the tide of identity theft crimes. Gartner analysts said banks and other FSPs must be pressured by consumers and lobbyists to proactively back efforts such as the U.S. Fair Credit Reporting Act, which would cover security and accuracy of personal financial information, which would make it easier for victims to report a crime to financial institutions.

"Most importantly, however, banks and FSPs must implement solutions that effectively screen for application fraud, so they don't wrongfully extend credit to identify thieves," said Avivah Litan, vice president and research director for the Gartner Group. "Without industry prevention efforts, consumers whose identities have been stolen will continue to bear the brunt of social and indirect economic costs."

Even something as simple as this would be an improvement; whenever a credit grantor extends credit to an impostor after the victim has placed a fraud alert on the credit file, a stiff penalty should be assessed.

As the hemming and hawing and thumb twiddling continues by those who can make the much needed changes to protect our identities, the numbers will continue to climb, and they're already jaw-dropping. As a reminder:

- Over the past five years, 27.3 million Americans had their identities stolen. Last year alone, nearly 10 million people were victims of identity theft, and the number of people who discovered misuse of their personal information has increased 41 percent.

- Remember the report from the California Public Interest Research Group (CalPIRG)? They found the typical identity-theft victim spends 175 hours actively trying to resolve the problems caused by the theft. Problems include clearing up credit reports, filling out and submitting affidavits and dealing with lawyers.

  If it happens to you, do you think your credit card company and bank will clean up the mess? Think again. Instead, think of your busy schedule. Where will you find the time to straighten things out? What fun things will you be forced to give up? The time you set aside to kick back and unwind? Your lunches and coffee breaks? Your child's soccer games and school performances? Your vacation and sick days? (Granted, if it happens to you, you'll feel quite ill.)

- Identity theft victims pay $500 on average to clear their name while serious thefts pay an average of $1,200.

  That's just the average. It can be much worse. Remember the

nightmare Retired Army Lt. Colonel John Stevens faced? He spent over $6,000 in legal fees trying to repair his credit.

What will you be forced to forego up to pay for it? Money set aside for a new car, college or your retirement?

- *Privacy & American Business* estimates one in six adults have had their identities used by someone else since 1990.

Think About It:

When was the last time you checked your credit report? When was the last time you balanced your checkbook or scrutinized your credit card statement?

Don't be lulled into a false sense of security thinking this is crime of hustle and bustle, large impersonal cities and that you are far removed and therefore immune. Even if your town is so devoid of crime and so peaceful you don't lock your car or the front door of your home, your name appears in numerous databases.

Maybe Steven Benke of Portage, Indiana didn't worry about identity theft. That is until he ended up in jail for crimes he didn't commit.

Remember Robert Calip, a victim from Washington State? He said it almost tore up his marriage.

What about Jane and her husband, both professionals living in Michigan? They were about to buy their first home when they found out their credit was shot because someone in Texas had used Jane's name and Social Security number to obtain numerous credit cards, a BMW, and a mortgage. It took them two years to clean up the mess.

What about the identity mill creating fake California, Georgia, Florida, Maine, Nevada, New Hampshire, New Jersey, Utah, Wisconsin and New York driver's licenses, birth certificates and Social Security cards? Could your name be on any of those documents?

The next time you're at a football game, camping trip, in church, or a seminar, look at three people to your left and three to your right.

The odds are at least one of you have been, are, or will be victims of identity theft and chances are you won't even know it until you receive a letter or a nasty phone call. It just might be while you're cheering on the home team, listening to a ghost story, reflecting on a sermon or applauding a speaker, someone may be playing havoc with your name and reputation.

Consider trying this experiment. Ask your co-workers or people in your neighborhood, at church or your next bridge or poker game if they've ever been a victim of identity theft. Since one in six people have, the results might alarm you. If by some fluke, all of the people you ask say no, you could be doing them a great service by alerting them since most don't know until they receive a nasty phone call, or apply for a loan.

Maybe it's time for us to follow the lead of Retired Army Lt. Colonel John Stevens. Remember what he said? "We're mad as hell and we're not going to take it anymore!" This needs to become every law-abiding citizen's fight song.

Until and unless there's a serious crackdown or we all become proactive against all the burgeoning identity theft schemes out there, we are at the mercy of the con men and women who will seemingly do anything—*anything*—to prolong their life of crime and live off the sweat of our brows.

Author's Note

The author of this book—who wishes to remain anonymous—has twice been a victim of identity theft: once when noticing a slew of mysterious charges to his credit card from a distant state he had never visited, the other time when his bank balance dropped dramatically after surrendering his ATM card to a person he thought was a bank officer during a bank merger.

SIDEBAR

CONFESSIONS OF AN IDENTITY THIEF

(FROM AN INTERVIEW ON NATIONAL PUBLIC RADIO)

Curador (not his real name) is an 18-year-old hacker from rural Wales who, one winter, stole an estimated 26,000 credit cards numbers from a group of e-commerce Web sites and posted the numbers, which belonged to people all over the world on the Web. After an ex-hacker tracked him down, he was arrested on, and charged under the United Kingdom's computer crime statute.

NPR: What kind of thrill do you get out of hacking? Is it sort of the New Age equivalent of sex, drugs and rock-and-roll?
CURADOR: I suppose you could call it that, in a way. After the first ten minutes, when I was waiting for the five and a half thousand credit cards I was to download from the first site. Certainly there was a great rush, so to speak. You do get a rush from doing it—definitely. There is a lot of adrenaline, if nothing else, while you're trying to track it down. I sometimes spent two days solid trying to do something without sleep, without anything, just constantly trying to do it.

NPR: What do computers give you back?
CURADOR: Computers are my career as well. I can get paid for doing the kind of work that I do. And you get a lot back in satisfaction, really, from writing programs and things like that, finding new ways of doing things.

NPR: But you're like a burglar who breaks into the houses just to see what's in there. You don't take anything. What's the point?
CURADOR: I think, obviously, I'm just a very nosey person. I'm like your nosey neighbor on steroids, basically. It can be interesting, because when you see into someone's computer, it gives you an idea of how they work, who they speak to, what they're interested in, whether they actually do any work, what their job is. You can see a lot of someone's life just from the contents of their PC. Some people even have correspondence with their family at home from their PCs, and so on. So it just depends.

NPR: What's your fascination with credit card numbers?
CURADOR: They're a good choice. People don't like other people to know they have their credit card numbers.

NPR: That's because people that get them use them to buy stuff.
CURADOR: Yes.

NPR: Is that why you were getting them?
CURADOR: No, I didn't try and buy anything with them that wasn't refunded. There are loads of things I could've used them for. But I didn't. The whole point of it was the message.

NPR: And what was the message?
CURADOR: There are a lot of people out there who won't even safeguard their own safety, let alone the safety of their customers. At the end of the day, it's the fault of these companies. The buck does stop with them. But they're not even trying to protect their own business from that.

Don't be lulled into thinking what goes on overseas doesn't affect you in Anytown, USA. This is where the money is. Plus, we're only as far away as a couple of keystrokes, a poorly chosen password or doing business with a careless company.

FACTOIDS

Ten Things Anyone Can Find Out About You

1. Your current and previous address (from the U.S. Postal Service and credit bureaus)
2. Any criminal convictions (from court records)
3. Whether you have a professional license (from licensing agencies)
4. Whether you have filed lawsuits or been a defendant in a lawsuit (from court records)
5. If you've had speeding tickets, drunken driving convictions or other black marks on your driving record (from the drivers' license bureau)
6. What cars, trucks, boats and planes you own (from state motor vehicle records)
7. Whether you have filed for bankruptcy or had liens placed against your property (from court records)
8. What you have pledged as collateral for bank loans (from Universal Commercial Code filings, usually in county recorder's offices)
9. What pieces of real estate you own and how much you paid (from county tax records)
10. Whether there's a warrant out for your arrest (from court records and police agencies)

All of this is available from companies such as www.USSearch.com which markets its services to businesses and individuals.

Common Ways Identity Thieves Use Your Personal Information

- They call your credit card issuer and, pretending to be you, ask to change the mailing address on your credit card account. The imposter then runs up charges on your account. Because your bills are being sent to the new address, it may take some time before you realize there's a problem.
- They open a new credit card account, using your name, date of birth and Social Security number. When they use the credit card and don't pay the bills, the delinquent account is reported on your credit report.
- They establish phone or wireless service in your name.
- They open a bank account in your name and write bad checks on that account.
- They file for bankruptcy under your name to avoid paying debts they've incurred under your name, or to avoid eviction.
- They counterfeit checks or debit cards, and drain your bank account.
- They buy cars by taking out auto loans in your name.

Source: SEC

THE TOP 11 CATEGORIES OF CONSUMER FRAUD COMPLAINTS IN 2002

1. **IDENTITY THEFT - 43 PERCENT**
2. Internet Auctions - 13 percent
3. Internet Services and Computer Complaints - 6 percent
4. Advance Fee Loans and Credit Protection - 5 percent
5. Shop-at-Home/Catalog Sales - 5 percent
6. Foreign Money Offers - 4 percent
7. Prizes/Sweepstakes and Lotteries - 4 percent
8. Business Opportunity and Work-at-Home Plans - 3 percent
9. Telephone Services - 2 percent
10. Health Care - 2 percent
11. Magazines and Buyers Clubs - 2 percent

Source: SEC

Most Common Identity Frauds

	Percent of Cases*
Credit Card	42%
Phone or Utilities	22%
Bank	17%
Employment-related Benefits	9%
Benefits of Government Documents	8%
Attempted Identity Theft	8%
Loans	6%
Other	16%

*Does not total 100% as most victims experience more than one act of fraud.

Source: SEC

BIBLIOGRAPHY

Articles and Reports

"14 Ways to Stop Identity Theft Cold, *MSN Money* (By Bankrate.com), April 21, 2003.

"Citibank Warns Customers of Email Scam," *Reuters*, August 19, 2003.

"Federal Trade Commission Identity Theft Survey Report," September 2003.

"Federal Trade Commission Overview of Identity Theft Program," October 1998–2003.

Ferrell, Keith, "Identity Theft Soars, but It's Still a Low-Tech Crime," *TechWeb News*, July 23, 2003

Foley, Linda, "Identity Theft and the Workplace," *IHRIM.link* magazine, February/March 2003.

"Gartner Says Identity Theft Is Up Nearly 80 Percent," (Press Release), July 21, 2003.

Givens, Beth, "ID Theft—A Rapidly Growing Crime that Scars its Victims," *Consumer Action*, Spring 2000.

Heikkila, Pia, "Experts Predict Online ID Theft Epidemic, *Silicon.com*, November 21, 2000.

"ID Theft—Very 21st Century, Very Serious," *Silicon.com*, February 26, 2003.

"Identity Theft: The Impact on Seniors Prepared Statement of the Federal Trade Commission on Identity Theft: The Impact on Seniors," Before the Senate Special Committee on Aging, Washington, D.C., July 18, 2002.

"ID Theft," *Consumer Reports*, October 2003.

"Internet Guide to Safety, Privacy and Security," National Consumer League Brochure.

Kotadia, Munir, "ID Theft Worsening," *Silicon.com*, July 22, 2003.

Legon, Jeordan, "'Phishing' Scams Reel in Your Identity," *CNN*, July 22, 2003.

Livingston, Brian, "Identity Theft Crisis," *eWeek*, August 11, 2003.

Maddux, Stan, "Stolen Identity Puts Man in Jail," *Gary Post-Tribune*, Feb. 14, 2003.

McCue, Andy, "Russian Hackers Behind Fake PayPal Email Scam?," *Silicon.com*, July 11, 2003.

McGuire, David, "FTC, Business Renew Fight Against ID Theft," *Washington Post*, September 3, 2003.

"Policing Privacy: Law Enforcement's Response To Identity Theft," California Public Interest Research Group (CalPIRG), May 1, 2003.

Pollack and James May, "Authentication Technology: Identity Theft and Account Takeover," *FBI Law Enforcement Bulletin,* June 2002.

"*Privacy & American Business* Survey Finds 33.4 Million Americans Victims Of ID Theft; Consumer Out-Of-Pocket Expenses Total $1.5 Billion A Year," (Press Release), *Privacy & American Business,* a publication of the Center for Social & Legal Research, July 30, 2003.

"Regulators Urge Identity Theft Prevention," Associated Press, August 12, 2003.

Roberts, Paul, "FBI Warns of Spike in Identity Thefts," *PC World – IDG News Service,* July 21, 2003.

"Safeguarding Your Identity," *Liberty Lines,* Fall 2003.

"Scams & Consumer Alerts," Identity Theft Resource Center, October 2003.

Stengle, Jamie, "Scams are After Black Elderly Identity Theft," *Associated Press,* September 19, 2000.

Testimony: House Ways and Means, Social Security Number Subcommittee, July 10, 2003.

"Social Security Number and Identity Theft," U.S. House of Representatives: House Financial Services Testimony, June 24, 2003.

Books

Anonymous, James Jennings, Michael Connor, *How to Create a New Identity,* Citadel Press, 1987.

Charrett, Sheldon, *Modern Identity Changer: How To Create And Use A New Identity For Privacy And Personal Freedom,* Paladin Press, 1997.

Charrett, Sheldon, *Secrets of a Back Alley ID Man: Fake ID Construction Techniques of the Underground,* Paladin Press, 2001.

Ernst, Carl R., (Editor), Michael L. Sankey (Editor), *Public Records Online: The National Guide to Private and Government Online Sources of Public Records,* Facts on Demand Press, 1997.

Forge, Max, *How to Make Driver's Licenses and Other ID on Your Home Computer,* Loompanics Unlimited, 1999.

Greenwald, Jesse M., *Document Fraud and Other Crimes of Deception,* Loompanics Unlimited, 1997.

Hammond, Robert, *Identity Theft: How to Protect Your Most Valuable Asset,* Career Press, 2003.

King, Dennis, *Get the Facts on Anyone* (2nd Ed.), Hungry Minds, Inc, 1995.

McKeown, Kevin, Dave Stern (Contributor), *Your Secrets Are My Business,* Plume, 2000.

Newman, John Q, *Identity Theft: The Cybercrime of the Millennium,* Loompanics Unlimited, 1999.

Vacca, John, *Identity Theft,* Prentice Hall PTR, 2002.

Web Sites of Interest

Consumer Action
http://www.Consumer-Action.org

Federal Trade Commission
http://www.FTC.gov

Identity Theft Resource Center (ITRC)
http://www.idtheftcenter.org/index.shtml

Internet Fraud Watch
http://www.fraud.org/internet/intset.htm

Junkbusters
http://www.junkbusters.com

National Consumer League
http://www.nclnet.org

National Fraud Information Center
http://www.fraud.org

Privacy & American Business (Center for Social & Legal Research)
http://www.pandab.org
http://www.PrivacyExchange.org

Privacy Rights Clearinghouse
http://www.privacyrights.org/identity.htm

Silicon.com
http://www.silicon.com

Urban Legends (Snopes)
http://www.snopes2.com

INDEX

NOTES